Abundance
Born of Poverty

KRISTEN MÄGIS

ISBN-13: 978-1986646611

ISBN-10: 1986646610

CreateSpace Independent Publishing Platform, North Charleston, SC

DEDICATION

I dedicate this book

to Michelle, whose spirit and will to create her art persevered through poverty and homelessness;

to Kathy who I pray will learn finally that she is love worthy;

to us all that we may step into our birthright as warriors of love for life;

and to my children, that they discover the strength within their souls when they encounter dark moments in their lives.

CONTENTS

FORWARD

'Who are you, really?' Gaia asks, 'and, why are you here?'

'I am,' I start. 'I chose to incarnate into this human form. Yet, the currents of this life throw me off balance, turn me upside down. So, when finally I face the sky and fill my lungs with chi, I have forgotten who I am and why I am here.'

Gaia smiles, 'The challenges, joys, the questions, and yes, even the pains, are the stage and setting of the play you write as you journey through this life. They are divine gifts for your ascension, clues to help you remember, opportunities to fulfill the promise of who you are.'

'Yet,' Gaia reminds, 'who you become and whether you fulfill your promise is not preordained. Rather, you create yourself each moment of your life. You are the playwright, the producer and the lead actress. We await the words you will write on the blank page that is each new day in your life. Always remember as you journey this life that Spirit walks with you, setting the stage, offering support and loving you.'

The stories in this book share recent passages on my journey through this life. I pray they will inspire your journey to create who you are and to fulfill the promise into which you were born.

Upon my return from a year in Viet Nam, I turned inward to discern Spirit's calling for the next phase of my life. My calling, Spirit counseled, was to write a book with the title, *Abundance Born of Poverty*. I accepted the calling, unaware Spirit had already set me upon a journey that would turn my world inside out, and in the process, untangle the apparent contradiction of this term, Abundance Born of Poverty.

As this frightening journey unfolded, a story of love and oppression was born, titled *I Am Love Worthy*. Then, an audacious spirit introduced herself, demanding that I give voice to her terrible message. She is *Cailleach*.

Just three months later, Spirit abruptly set me upon yet another passage. My heart failed. A story issued from this journey, *Strength Born of Weakness*.

1 ABUNDANCE BORN OF POVERTY

THE QUIET VOICE RINGS CLEAR

After months of quiet, prayer and listening,
  Spirit finally made its request known to me.

Spirit requested that I transform my passion
  vis-à-vis poverty, food security and water rights
  into a force that inspires my actions and decisions.
  Spirit asked that I give voice to all who live in poverty.

I am to write a book entitled, 'Abundance Born of Poverty'.

I accept the invitation, absolutely.
  I will portray the face of poverty,
  make heard the voice of poverty.

I believe that when poverty is given a face,
  love will conquer ignorance, fear and hate.

Love will restore our understanding that
  we are all ONE.

When one of us suffers, every soul is aggrieved.
  When one of us offers love, we are all blessed.

I cannot see the journey whereby this calling will unfold.
  But I trust that Spirit has set the course, and will reveal
  the path and heading so that I might fulfill my promise.

Spirit has graced me with a calling.
  I am blessed. I am so very blessed.

STREET SLEEPER

Yesterday, poverty presented itself to me,
　dressed in the garb of a friend and teacher.

Her soul's sorrow leapt at me from a block away.
　She pulled for breath, but life portioned it in small gasps.

The migraine presented yesterday,
　but she had no medicine to stop its rampage.

Still, she came to work, for she could not afford to lose the
　$300/week upon which she and her partner barely subsist.

Sometime during that migraine, her glasses broke,
　leaving her sightless and without recourse to fix them.

Nor could she drive to an eye doctor, because
　she can't afford the fee to renew her driver's license.

She drives to the street where she sleeps, then to work,
　ever fearful of having her home-on-wheels impounded.

Meanwhile, unbeknownst to her, a vendor withdrew money
　from her bank account, after she had canceled the service.

The overdraft cost her another $35, and triggered a cascade
　of bounced checks that triggered more overdrafts and fees.

So, she drove to work with a migraine and no glasses,
　and no money for dinner.

LIFE ON THE STREETS

My friend is starting a business to break her out of poverty.
　But, she doesn't have startup capital to purchase supplies.

She found a nonprofit that offers micro loans to women
　who live in poverty to finance small business ventures.

Then, she learned that to qualify for the loan,
　she could not have any outstanding debt.

The problem is, through an ill-fated event,
　she went into debt to the tune of $200.

Her choice: pay the debt, eat, or make her van loan payment.
　The van payment is paid, the bank waits and dinner is soup.

And the poorest-of-poor can't access the very resources
　intended to assist them to find their way out of poverty.

YOU DON'T SEE ME

I saw an elder homeless woman, resting on a bench.
  She glanced at me, filling my mind with her story.

'I am here...see me?
  Look down. Here I am, sitting on the bench.
  I live behind the facade of the *American Dream*.'

'I don't blame you for not wanting to look.
  I wouldn't either. I wouldn't want to see the shame,
  the failure that I am. I wouldn't want to see me.'

'Yet, I live with this conundrum...I must eat.
  And, I must find a place to relieve myself,
  for I cannot stop my bodily functions...much as
  I know that would make us both more comfortable.'

'And, I must sleep...somewhere. I must sleep.
  But, this has all become so hard, you know.'

'The night is dangerous on the streets,
  so I must stay awake at night. It is,
  you know, my survival.'

'But then, whilst asleep in my car the next day,
  I was roused by the tapping on my window of
  the policeman with the billy-club, who told me,'

*"Wake up! Sleeping in your car during the day
is against the law!"*

'I remember, long ago, living in a house.
  It had a bed and I slept at night. And it had a
  bathroom where I could care for myself in private.'

'I never imagined that I would wake each morning wondering
  where I could go to the bathroom, if I would be allowed in
  the bathroom at the store, or if I might be kicked out
  because my clothes were too dirty and smelly.'

'I never imagined that financial collapse would be
  such a cascade of loss, or that one slip could
  put me back...again...and again...and again.'

'And yet, here I sit on this street corner,
  in the rain and in my humiliation.'

'And, you don't see me.'

AND SO, THE STORY BEGINS

Delighted beyond measure,
  I embraced my calling to write
  the book, *Abundance Born of Poverty*.

I had no idea what it meant, but
  knew from experience that Spirit
  would offer the wisdom and words.

I began in earnest to share the
  plight of people living in poverty,
  to expose the scourge that is poverty.

What I didn't understand is that
  my enlightenment was to emerge
  from living the story I was to share.

I had lived on the edge for 13 years.
  I believed the difficulties were over.
  The future was bright. I was primed.

Bolstered by my work in Vietnam,
  I anticipated securing work quickly,
  launching the next chapter of my life.

Two years later, I lost my housing.
  I had $1,000, no work, no income.
  The unthinkable had become reality.

Abundance Born of Poverty was inspired
  by others who struggled with poverty.
  It was born of my descent into poverty.

This story shares the unrelenting ravages
  of poverty on one's mind, body and soul,
  and the steady hand of Spirit through it all.

Three years later, I am still in awe
  at the wisdom Spirit shared about
  this complex and essential concept,

  Abundance Born of Poverty.

THINGS NOT MEANT FOR ME

There is a saying,

'Only three things matter,
　how much you loved,
　how gently you lived,
　and how gracefully you let go
　of things not meant for you.'

Funny I should come upon this quote just now.
　The level of emotive clash going on inside me
　advises me that these words are meant for me.

So,
　reticently casting off my favored
　'woe-is-me' mask, I look inside.

'Things not meant for you...'

Things not meant for me,
　I can count so many,
　just in the last months.

Spirit asks me to let go.
　But that is not enough.
　I must let go gracefully!

A high order for one sitting yet again
　among the shards of hope shattered.

So, to Spirit I turn,
　into my heart I fall,
　letting go, opening up.

Hoping
　I have the prudence to know
　what 'was not meant for me',
　as well as the grace to let it go.

Praying
　I will be given the prescience
　to know what is meant for me,
　and the wisdom to treat all that
　I find as the sacred gift that it is.

LETTING GO...WITH GRACE

Spirit is walking me through an intensive
  on a particular lesson, specifically, how to
  gracefully let go of things not meant for me.

Opportunities for me to explore, practice and learn
  from this lesson have been manifold in my life of late,
  so much so that I feel like an undersized boxer in the ring
  with a leviathan who delights in using me as a bouncing ball.

In this encounter with Spirit, I have marched diligently
  through my archetypical responses and rejoinders, from

'We're working this problem together,' to
'I can push harder,' to
'I'll try another approach, a new perspective,
  a different idea, any idea...' to
'It's getting scary down here!' to
'Damn it, Spirit! I'm gonna do this myself!' to
'I can't believe this is happening', and 'I'm still pissed!' to
'Oh my god! Is that the bottom approaching?!'

Despite my maneuvers, Spirit has provided no reprieve.
  I fancied that Spirit maintained the pressure because
  I'm ready for the lesson and I wouldn't yield or crack.

But then, I did crack.
  Threats to my livelihood proliferated without pause,
  layered one upon the other until, head spinning and
  tears in my eyes, it was all I could do to simply stand.

For days, I couldn't speak without dissolving into tears.
  Yet through it all, Spirit's words echoed through
  my mind like cosmic background noise,

'It matters how gracefully you let go
  of that which is not meant for you.'

So with each hope thwarted, I endeavor to the best
  of my ability to accept that it is not meant for me.
  Then, I attempt to let go of it, the hope, my hope.

But, what if the 'its' that aren't meant for you pile up
  into a mountain over which you can no longer see?
  Is there a point at which the mountain's magnitude
  suggests that your purpose and goals are mistaken?

There are so many dimensions to this lesson:
  recognizing when something really is not meant for you;
  acknowledging and accepting that it is not meant for you;
  staying close to the truth and not creating false storylines;
  letting go, despite your confusion or desire or incredulity;
  facing to the fore, free from attachment, to behold anew.

Let me describe what is happening before I melt
  into the pure abstractions of this contemplation.

The real-life story is this unthinkable year of futile job search.
  The 'its' are the multitude of posts for which I have applied.
  The 'not meant for yous' are the rejection notes and silences.

The mountain is constructed of rejected applications, from
  all sectors, stations and positions, even volunteer positions.
  Tell me, how is it that one can be rejected as a volunteer?!

So, facing a total shut out, I decided to pause and re-evaluate.
  I must be overlooking a cardinal principle, missing the point.
  I endeavored to re-visualize the panoptic core of this lesson.

Perhaps I'm not supposed to make a living with my doctorate.
  Perhaps I am meant to work a non-career job, so I can write.
  Perhaps my skills are not desired in the market, a no-brainer.

Perhaps I am intended to live poverty so I can truly know it.
  I am living in poverty, have no income, am watching as my
  savings vanish for simple living requisites - food and board.

When I accepted this calling, I trusted Spirit to present all that
  I needed to fulfill its purpose, but I never dreamed that living
  through poverty would be the passage to my enlightenment.

Yet here I sit, vacillating between incredulity, shock and belief,
  contemplating this lesson, trusting that it is necessary for the
  passage to my elucidation, wondering if and how I can learn
  the lesson offered, curious about the next steps on this path.

Gracefully letting go suggests an elegance, a gentleness,
  a compassionate heart, a 'go with God' frame of mind.
  It is loving even as one accepts that which is not to be.

I still have no employment or income.
  Nor do I have answers to my questions.
  But, I am learning what the questions are.
  For that, I am sincerely and humbly grateful.

ANOTHER CUT

Another rejection letter arrived today.

I know the rejections before opening them.
  I can feel the precision of the lacerations
  on a heart bleeding from many such cuts.

And I wonder,
  is there a point at which
  healing is no longer possible?

Because see, there are not enough jobs to go around,
  and there are so many ways in which I do not match.
  But, I try to figure them out, to find how I can match.

Twisting myself this way and that,
  donning this, dropping that,
  acting so, acting not.

THE COLLISION…OR IS IT COLLUSION…OF IRONIES

The irony of my trip to the food stamp office today
  does not evade me.

Nor does the fact that, on my journey to confront this
  next assault on my ego, I got lost in a neighborhood
  lined with brass fences and golden trees, sentinels for
  million-dollar homes tucked amidst ornamental lawns.

How is it, I wonder, that a woman with twenty years
  professional experience and three advanced degrees
  finds herself running this particular errand, this day?

I asked the food stamp worker about his day.
  He was thinking about food shopping.
  This irony also did not escape me.

So I sat, holding back the threatening deluge of tears,
  waiting for the worker to bring my food stamp card.
  Now, I wait for another week to find out if I qualify.

What does a family without food do during this wait?
  Are they standing on street corners with cardboard
  'Anything will help. God bless.' placards?

Or, are they at work and school, ignoring the hunger pains
  and hoping no one hears the incessant growling
  of stomachs filled only with emptiness?

MEASURE NOT

Measure not another from your own stead,
  for she walks not your path, but hers.
  And her steps follow the voice inside.

If you cannot hear the voice inside her,
  how can you measure her steps?

Listen, instead, for the voice in your heart.
  Live into that wisdom with grace and love.

RAISE YOUR VOICES

I've been contemplating.

What happens when your cash runs out
  and you still have no source of income?
  I see, on the streets of this city, people
  who know the answer to this question.

My pile of rejected job applications swells
  even as my rainy day savings disappear.
  And, I wonder if the path of poverty
  is not that which unfolds before me.

Yesterday, I dared step beyond the fear
  to consider this impossible potentiality.
  Burned by the advancing fire, I vowed
  that, should this be my path unfolding,

I will bring my pen and paper, and
  I will give voice to those standing
  on the street corners of this world,
  asking us to consider our humanity.

GOSSAMER

Gossamer
  is the substance of the wisdom I seek.

Imperceptible,
  I gaze through it without seeing it.

Intangible,
  fading in and out as a boat offshore.

Ethereal,
  a dimension unbound by the material.

ABUNDANCE BORN OF POVERTY

Abundance Born of Poverty.
  I cannot see it. I cannot fathom it.
  Perhaps, I am not looking hard enough.

Or perhaps, I am not open to the
  possibility that there really exists such
  a phenomenon as Abundance Born of Poverty.

I think that is the truth of it.

I cannot imagine how abundance can be born of poverty.
  I know poverty's bairn, relentless hardship and oppression.
  I am meeting its kinsmen, anguish, despair, suffering, fatigue.

Yet, Spirit requests that I write about abundance,
  the one experience I have not yet had with poverty.

Spirit, in its exasperatingly cryptic and nonsensical manner,
  asks for the seemingly impossible in the very moment that
  I feel least capable of, or interested in, deciphering its riddle.

THE BUGABOO WITH GNOSIS

The miracle of gnosis is knowing before learning.
  The challenge of gnosis is learning after knowing.
  Such is the enigma - Abundance Born of Poverty.

Usually, we learn our way into those things we come to know.
  The path to knowing is littered with inspiration, failures and
  rare epiphanies, all experienced en route to our illumination.

It is this journey that gifts us time to move through the many
  transformations necessary to assimilate the knowledge into
  our hearts and minds, and to integrate it into our daily walk.

Skipping this step is what creates the bugaboo with gnosis.
  The initial elation is followed by a disquieting realization
  that we know not the meaning of the wisdom revealed.

There is no shortcut to wisdom. We must experience life
  in full color to figure out the wisdom it offers to impart.
  This is no less true when we are bestowed with gnosis.

When gifted with gnosis, we live in the strange world of
  simultaneously holding the wisdom and having no idea
  what that wisdom means.

Abundance Born of Poverty.

THE COMPASSION

Silence fills my heart of late.
  Not a peaceful silence, no.
  It is a roaring, angry silence.

I do not feel therein the usual
  self doubt and discouragement.
  I just feel pure anger, pissed off.

Another wiser part of me knows that
  anger is not a quintessential sentiment.
  It is pure neither in substance nor form.

Rather it is a cloak, a shield, a weapon
  to turn outward when looking inward
  is too excruciating and laborious a task.

Yes, I know that.

Yet, sometimes I choose to linger
  in the raw, bleak, cold fusion of
  misgiving, bitterness, resentment.

It is an escape for me.
  While I linger in this space,
  I don't have to take responsibility.

I can build the rationale and justification
  for not moving forward or accepting life
  as it comes to me, for not living into my all.

And now, as I recall all this, I smile.
  I do want to step forward into life.
  I do want to live fully all of my life.

I do accept responsibility for my self.
  I can take another step into the mystery.
  I am willing to hold the inscrutable puzzle.

Then, another silence fills my heart.
  This silence is different than the first.
  It is peaceful, hopeful, tranquil. It is love.

It dissolves the anger, soothes my pain,
  envelops me with compassion and love,
  illumines the way, beckons me to the fore.

DANCE INTO TOMORROW

I am dancing without thinking about it.
  I am running, feet off the ground, flying into the dawn.
  I am energized by the potentialities, exploration, discoveries!

Then suddenly I remember,
  I cannot pay for the simple process of living.

My heart closes, my mind lurches, my soul retreats into dark.
  Ensconced in fear, I forget the possibilities, fall into despair.

And without adieu, the brilliance is snuffed out,
  eclipsed by the shroud of death that only fear can impart.
  Chi asphyxiated, ideas slaughtered, exploration terminated.

Turning humbly toward the light.
  Letting go the need to hide behind fear.
  Daring to face forward, to embrace the dance.
  Holding intention and faith as co-creators and bold.

Dancing in the mystery
  is for the courageous, the audacious, the extraordinary.
  And, it is for me...reluctant, awkward, regular, uncertain.
  Dance through your fear, even when you forget the steps.

Dance into tomorrow!

THE UNNAMABLE, THE ANIMATING FORCE

At times, the feeling of gratitude is so immense
  that I feel I will simply melt into the stars.

The gifts of Spirit are so rich, shared with elegance,
  and offered without expectation of recompense.

Gifted simply because.

So, I fall to my knees,
  tears glistening on my cheeks,
  the grace of God filling my heart,
  a sense of awe opening my soul
  to the ALL that is.

Thank you, Great Spirit, Creator,
  whatever your name is or is not,
  whatever space your fill or create,
  whatever form you are or are not.

Thank you.

LAY BARE THE AMERICAN DREAM

There's a story I've felt called to tell, but, I've been afraid,
  for the telling would permit that pitiless and harsh judge
  who is me to recount my faults, my ineptitude, my failure.

My private judge and jury expects that I, without question,
  will accept and condone its brutal and malicious verdicts
  as the uncontested and definitive characterization of me.

I do. But sometimes, I remember that the judgments
  are part of an American myth, a fallacious story that
  duplicitously indicts thousands of unsuspecting souls.

I embraced that story, studied the lessons carefully,
  those lessons that were indoctrinated in childhood,
  those lessons that define the limits of who I can be.

The story, 'I am responsible for the conditions of my life.
  If I try hard enough, study hard enough, work hard enough,
  I will secure recompense for my efforts. It's up to me alone.'

Sound familiar?
  Of course, it does.
  This is the American Dream.

These lessons permeated my life, fashioned my expectations.
  They were edified by my father, who lost all in a country
  ravaged by war, then realized his dreams in America.

I witnessed him live the story. I bought into it.
  I believed it. I presumed it was my story as well.
  So, I adhered wholeheartedly to the wise directives.

I worked hard. I studied hard. I believed...hard.
  I worked harder, longer, unrelentingly, passionately.
  I accepted success and failure as mine, and mine alone.

But then the story changed, the plot became indecipherable.
  Despite years of work and education, I couldn't find work.
  I engaged all my well-honed skills in my search, to no avail.

So, after careful evaluation of my circumstances,
  I decided that my skills were no longer marketable.
  I went back to school to acquire new knowledge that
  would help me to realize that elusive American Dream.

Five years later, after raising my children in poverty
  and earning a doctorate, I attached five-page letters to

13

five-page vitaes and sent them to countless employers,
none of whom considered my résumé worth pursuing.

I had new skills though, that when added to my previous
repertoire, shaped a professional of significant potential.
I persisted in job search, proving myself over and again
until finally, I was given a part-time, short-term, contract.

Let me stop for a moment to sit with the irony of the fact
that after 20 years of professional experience and three
advanced degrees culminating in a doctorate, I had to
demonstrate my skills, just to land a part-time contract.

Did you know that only 3% of women...in the world...
earn their doctorates?

I say this not for the purpose of self-aggrandizement.
Believe me, I have internalized the American fiction
too deeply to presume I am better than anyone else.

I say it to underscore the absurdity of these circumstances.

I made the most of the opportunity, consulting internationally,
working with developing countries and the United Nations,
researching, publishing, teaching, presenting professionally.

That was 16 months ago. And, what have I been doing since?
I have been looking for work, every day, searching for work.
And mind you, I bring considerable expertise to the charge.

I have copious and detailed charts, plans and processes.
I have a list of 100+ jobs for which I have submitted
carefully crafted letters and lengthy, in-depth vitaes.

You want to know how to look for work? I can teach you.
You want to know how to secure a job? I don't know.
The formula to realize the American Dream isn't working.

It must be my fault, my deficiencies, me.
It could never be the American Dream.
To consider such would be unthinkable.

Now, I am a frugal person. I live simply and carefully.
I recycle and reuse, shop at secondhand stores,
and purchase only food and necessities.

I relinquished 95% of my things and rented out my home.
I could no longer afford to live there, or even to sell it.
I lived in rented rooms these last three years.

I splurge only rarely and only for my children and grandson.
I have lived seven years without health insurance because
I need the $700 per month to pay for necessities like food.

Of the many blessings I have been gifted, a strong body
is one for which I can't even start to give enough thanks.
It has carried me through these years, and failed me not.

Yet, aware of how easily I could fall from the meager table
of opulent-poverty to destitution, I changed my lifestyle.
I stopped kayaking because I might have an accident and
incur bills that a lifetime of payments would not reconcile.

Then, I stopped eye exams and switched eye doctors to find
one that would fill an old prescription without requiring
that I undergo and reimburse them for another exam.

Regrettably, the new doctor now necessitates an exam, for
which I don't have the money. So I live in hopes that my
glasses will last indefinitely and my eyesight won't change.

Then, a tooth broke. No dental insurance, no dental care.
Years later, while in Viet Nam, I invested my earnings
in dental care. Dentists are affordable in Viet Nam.

Later, the filling fell out and another tooth broke.
Back to square one, two broken teeth.
No, that's square one minus one.

Quick interlude...
I tell this story not to get your pity. For god's sake, no!
I tell it because I am called to give voice to the voiceless.

Despite everything I've gone through this decade,
I've been gifted in myriad ways through my life,
which has fortified me for this journey into loss.

I'm telling this story for those who haven't been so gifted.
I'm telling it for them and I'm telling it for every one of us.
For you see, material poverty is the child of spiritual poverty.

Material poverty cannot exist without a community that
condones and supports it. While material poverty exists,
all in the community suffer the plague of spiritual poverty.

There is a scourge in our midst,
but it is not the poor among us.

It is the fraudulent story that entraps us all in its brutal grip,
  distorts our perception of reality, turns us against our own,
  creates alienation, and rewards collusion with its chicanery.

This is not about pity, charity or Christian or civic duty.
  This is about waking up to the reality in which we live.
  It is about exposing the deceit and changing the story.

I believe we are smart and industrious and compassionate.
  But, we must expose the story's false pretense so we can act.
  For, we are all ONE, and the fate of one is the destiny of all.

I pray we gather the will to examine the story's plot,
  and to re-write the story so that all may be blessed
  on the shared journey of our souls through this life.

DETACHMENT AND WILD ABANDON

These words, Spirit shares with me.

'Witness, learn. Discover possibilities.
  Explore, imagine. Withhold judgment.
  Spread your wings. Reclaim your voice.'

Spirit invites me forth, reminding me
  that I have only started the journey to
  welcome wisdom into my heart and soul.

So, blessed with Spirit's healing and promise,
  I set again on the path, using my search for work
  to learn more deeply the lessons presented by Spirit.

I have something important to learn about detachment,
  as well as the merging of detachment with wild abandon.
  At first, this seems an oxymoron, an indecipherable puzzle.

Yet, I believe that what appears impossible is often not that,
  but rather my failure to see beyond self-imposed limitations.
  So, I hold the idea, detachment merged with wild abandon.
  And, I wonder how it fits with the words Spirit shares.

'Witness, learn. Discover possibilities.
  Explore, imagine. Withhold judgment.
  Spread your wings. Reclaim your voice.'

MY DESCENT

I am endeavoring to embrace an alternative way of thinking.
I glimpse the source from which the epiphany will emerge.
I feel the words, but as my fingers alight on the keyboard,
they are gone, and the revelation disappears into the mist.

I believe that I am creating the mist. I am blocking the Divine.
The mist issues from my inability to grasp my circumstances.
I am incredulous at the seemingly immutable fact of my life.
My mind is stuck in a perpetual cycle of incomplete analysis.

What stone sits unturned? What misunderstandings remain?
What silence must be held? What lessons await explication?
Seeking the precept that permits release from my purgatory.

But for the hemorrhaging of my funds, all remains unchanged.
I list the strategies and tactics alongside the hundreds of jobs.
They all sport the word 'Denied' stamped in bold, red letters.

My brain is overtaxed by circular, incomplete investigations.
My heart is gripped by fear of impending disaster, by fears
that I am unworthy, a failure, unqualified, insufficient, OR
I am unneeded in this economy, a resource sink, disposable.

This all perplexes my befuddled brain, strikes fear in my heart.
A riot is incited of inexplicable questions, manic analyses
and desperate conclusions, painting a bizarre scene,
terror tainted by drunken, livid irrationality.

All my life is superimposed on this backdrop.
Circumstance and people are seen, not as they are,
but as scenes and characters in a preordained narrative;
one written and produced by me; culminating in my demise.

I cannot celebrate other people's lives or their good fortune.
I feel envious of their destiny; contempt when I learn that
my knowledge eclipses theirs; chagrin and humiliation that
they were given the jobs for which I cannot get interviews.

Poisoned by this toxic cocktail of resentment and bitterness,
I act with a foul mix of self-disgust and bombastic theatrics.
My behavior leaves a caustic bile in my mouth that despoils
delicate hopefulness, and nourishes the burgeoning despair.

All folds in on itself, creates a lethal quagmire out of which
I cannot climb, or see, or feel, or act, or breath, or believe.
I can't find the bottom of this pit, can't stop from digging.

It is natural to resist seeing oneself as superfluous, unwanted.
  It is natural to defend oneself from this horrifying prospect.
  So, I forge villains out of strangers and those whom I envy.

This is one route from fear to hate.
  There are many paths from fear to hate.
  But, they all end in destruction of the soul.

Do you recognize this story?
  Can you name the players?
  Can you describe the plot?

This is the rotting, fetid cesspool, the primordial sludge,
  the undifferentiated mass out of which we must climb.
  Like an unstoppable landslide, fear begets anger which
  sires contempt, jealousy, bitterness, resentment, hate...

This is what holds us back from seeing our potential,
  from recognizing our connections and our oneness,
  from quitting our perilous flirtation with extinction.

Spirit reaches into my insanity, saying, 'The way forward
  is love, incomprehensible, transcendent, whole-hearted
  love.'

SPIRIT, MATERIAL, SPIRIT, SPIRIT, SPIRIT

Sometimes, this reality feels so dense,
  like formed and unformed is out of balance,
  like the material is crowding out the potential.

The material bogs me down, slows my motion,
  obstructs my vision, obliterates my perception,
  severs my bond to the real, the ALL, isolates me.

So, I spin faster and faster,
  to shake loose material encumbrances,
  to disembody my energy so that I might
  settle once again into exquisite, pure being.

I witness the material molder into a primordial mass.
  I feel gravity dissipate, let loose its terrene authority.
  Light all round, material melting back into potential.
  Feeling again the liberty to breath, to soar, to know.

Spirit, Spirit, Spirit

DARK NIGHT OF THE SOUL

This week, my teacher assigned us to
  proclaim, 'Hallelujah' in midst of suffering.
  This, I believed, is a Spirit-inspired entreaty to life.

That was the theory and my inspiration.
  And now, as another dark night descends on
  my soul, I am called to sing, Hallelujah, even as I cry.

I listen to Leonard Cohen's, *Hallelujah*,
  a thousand times because I cannot bring
  such a word of hope and praise to my lips.

Hallelujah, Hallelujah, Hallelujah!

They are cold, hungry and thirsty.
  Warm them, feed them, hold the holy
  gift of pristine water to their parched lips.

Hallelujah, Hallelujah, Hallelujah!

Reach to the depths of your immortal soul.
  Find there the treasures gifted your mortal being.
  Shower the world with those gifts..with wild abandon.

Hallelujah, Hallelujah, Hallelujah!

I don't know the tune, but I feel the rhythm.
  I don't know words, yet they appear on the page.
  I can't see the path, but each stride lights the next step.

Hallelujah, Hallelujah, Hallelujah!

Wretched, hopeless, frightened, alone.
  The heaviness of our hearts draws us ever
  more thoroughly into the dark, the holy dark.

Hallelujah, Hallelujah, Hallelujah?

Wealth beyond measure concealing empty hearts.
  The ravenous, bottomless abyss of avarice and desire
  turning souls stone-cold, imploding life on itself, laughing.

Hallelujah, Hallelujah, Hallelujah?

The darkest nights of our souls.
  Humankind, scourge upon the earth.
  People, the answer, the Hallelujah, the hope.

Hallelujah, Hallelujah, Hallelujah!

IT'S STILL NOT OVER

Mourning, weeping all day
  I cannot stop the tears.

They stream from me
  like a dam broken.

But it's not a dam.
  It is my heart.

Trying,
  to adapt,
  to be creative,
  to go with the flow,
  to try different things.

Futile prayers for a release
  that never materializes.

Dreams of possibilities
  inspire hopefulness.

Life, a skillful thief,
  steals the dreams.

My heart,
  impoverished,
  desolate, hollow,
  deserted, hardened,
  now a thousand shards.

'breathe, breathe, breathe...'

'Turn the corner.
  Take another step.'

'It is not over.
  It is far from over.'

A MOTHER'S EMBRACE

My mother comes to me frequently these days.
  On my knees, head bowed, tears flowing.

She comes to care for her daughter.
  I weep. She holds me closely.

She embraces me. I cry.

The pain, the fear, the loss
  dissolve and float away.

I feel safe. I am warm.
  I am loved, wanted.

She stays. I cry.

She lifts my heart,
  gazes into my soul.

Healing, quiet, peace.
  No answers, only love.

My mother loves. I weep.

HALLELUJAH

Tears cascading, heart breaking, alone.
  Hallelujah, Hallelujah, Hallelujah.

Embrace my soul, for I fear it is dying.
  Hallelujah, Hallelujah, Hallelujah.

And then, I will vanish into oblivion.
  Hallelujah, Hallelujah, Hallelujah.

'There is no oblivion or inferno, only love.'
  Hallelujah, Hallelujah, Hallelujah.

'I hear you. I feel your anguish. I love you.'
  Hallelujah, Hallelujah, Hallelujah.

'You do not need answers, simply prayer.'
  Hallelujah, Hallelujah, Hallelujah.

'Your tears are precious. You are cherished.'
  Hallelujah, Hallelujah, Hallelujah.

'You are beauty. You are light. I AM here.'
  Hallelujah, Hallelujah, Hallelujah.

21

EAGLE

White Wolf Woman drew nigh.
  'Why did you take leave of me?!
  You have been gone so long,' say I.

'You sent me away, dear one,' she smiles.
  She wraps her arm around me and we walk.
  The field before us turns to shimmering gold.

Eagle falls from the sky,
  hovers alongside my face,
  takes my eyes with its talons.

I am wrapped in a black shroud.
  My body is lifted above the mass,
  gently passed from one to the other.

Until at last, we arrive at the precipice.
  They cast my body to the wind.
  Darkness, falling, alone…

'Eagle!' I scream.
  'Why did you steal my eyes?!'

Eagle swoops beneath me,
  catches my catapulting body,
  lays me in warm, down feathers,
  surrounds me with powerful wings.

White Wolf Woman
  holds me in her arms.
  Her tears flow into the
  holes that once bore my eyes.

'I stole your eyes,' avers Eagle,
  'because you are seeking wisdom
  and defining reality outside yourself.'

'The material world is only part of reality.
  It is but a reflection, a shadow of true reality.
  Blinded, you must seek wisdom inside yourself.'

'Seek the ALL within your heart.
  Trust there is more than you realize.
  Know that ALL is created by the Sacred.

THESE THINGS THAT HAPPEN

This is life.
  Things happen.
  How?

I called them in before I was born.
  I call them with my thoughts.
  Random occurrences…

In the end, 'how' doesn't matter,
  because here they are,
  these things that happen.

They gather before me,
  request my attention,
  await my response.

Always, I am offered a choice in
  my response to these things.
  Of this, I am fully certain.

So, these things that happen
  are awaiting my response,
  and I, well, I choose…

to live into them,
  to explore their essence,
  to find grace in and through them.

I choose
  to draw from the Sacred life-force,
  to allow the breath to course all through
  my frightened heart, my confounded mind.

I will ask of these things that happen,
  'What gifts of enlightenment bring you?'
  'What do you request that I bequest to life?'

These things that happen,
  introductions to the next step
  on this journey through life to life.

THESE THINGS, GIFTS UNFOLDING

Finally, turning my life-force from
  what I believed was supposed to be.
  I realize now, these things that happen
  are portents of the forthcoming journey.

What I thought was supposed to be
  was only an image in my mind,
  a reflection of another's path,
  a wandering of my fancy.

So, these things that happen,
  I shall welcome you now,
  appeal to your wisdom.

I welcome, thankfully,
  the mystery, the journey,
  its beginning and unfolding.

THE EPIPHANY THAT WANTS TO BE BORN

I decided that the worst thing that can happen to me
  is not that I end up homeless or without sustenance.

The worst thing that can happen is that
  I turn this life circumstance against me.

The self-questioning, self-loathing, self-deprecation.
  All of this epitomizes the worst that could happen.

I really am not what the world reflects to me.
  I really AM the light radiating from within.

The life circumstances are bearable.
  I can handle whatever comes to me.

I am resourceful, frugal, insightful, smart, well-balanced.
  I have internal strength that nourishes and sustains me.

What I cannot bear is the acceptance and internalization
  of society's judgment for the circumstances of my life.

Somehow, I must dispel this false impression from my mind,
  for it turns me against myself, denies the blessing that I am.

There it is, the gift, the message Spirit wants me to absorb.
  I can almost feel it, want to believe it, am reaching for it.

ALONE

A man who runs a pantry to feed the hungry shared a story
of a homeless gentleman's description of homelessness.

'Homelessness is not about a loss of resources,' he explained.
Homelessness is about the loss of friends and community.'

With full bellies, Portland's homeless returned to the streets.
I studied the pad inscribed with notes from our dialogue.

The homeless man's insight leapt at me, dagger in hand,
malice throbbing in anticipation, ravenous for the kill.

Panic rose, bile in my throat, as I searched for an eraser.
Desperate to eliminate the harsh reality from my life.

The words erased from the page, I collapsed in horror,
bile filling my mouth and heart, panic choking me.

The words emblazoned on my heart, in my life,
seething, breeding venom, stinking...

SPIRITUAL POVERTY

It occurs to me that I can't explore material poverty
without also contemplating spiritual poverty.

In fact, I wonder...

Would material poverty exist
in a world of spiritual wealth?

I DON'T TAKE ANYTHING FOR GRANTED ANYMORE

I guess that's really only partially true.
I take for granted that water will stream
from the faucet, and that it will be potable.

I take for granted that I will eat on this day,
and that the food will be nourishing and filling.
I take for granted that the choices I make are mine.

The things that I do not take for granted are whether
I will have food when my savings are depleted,
or a bed in a warm house on which to sleep.

I no longer take those things for granted.
There is no future guarantee of them.
But, I am grateful for them now.

HIGH STAKES AND SOUL CHOICES

The stakes are high.

I have committed to a strategy for action.
  I made the plan with a dearth of information
  simply because limited information was available.

I have committed my remaining savings
  to execute this plan in the best possible way.
  All my actions are aligned to accomplish my plan.

There is no guarantee this plan will work.
  All I know is that when I complete the plan,
  I will have new skills and my funds will be gone.

The stakes are high.

I could say that I have no other choice
  which would be one way to interpret life,
  but I favor the idea that there are still choices.

I choose to believe this situation is an
  invitation to embark on the next phase
  of the journey I dreamed for this lifetime.

It's not potential homelessness or hunger
  that challenge, threaten and jeopardize me.
  The danger is my fear of those potentialities.

How will I respond to that trepidation?
  Will I give it my every breath and future?
  Or will I love it and follow my chosen path?

Each day, I am presented that question.
  Each day, I choose and live my response.
  Each day, I get to choose and create my life.

So, this is the stage, and I am the author,
  creator, actress, audience and commentator.
  My life, my choice...What shall I write this day?

NOTE TO SELF

The world you perceive with your senses
  is simply the stage upon which you act.

What is important is the world inside,
  how you respond to it in your heart,
  who you decide to be on that stage.

KRISTEN MÄGIS

MY FRIEND, MY INSPIRATION

My dear friend rejoiced in recounting
  her newest feat in eating 'on a dime'.

She can create a complete meal for
  her partner and herself for $2.80.

For the feat of eating in the most healthy way possible,
  I love my friend.

For the daily accomplishment of surviving in her van,
  I love my friend.

For rising every day to endure yet another challenge,
  I love my friend.

I am thankful for the opportunity
  to share some small part of life with her,
  to learn from her the wisdom-born-of-poverty.

She inspires me to practice
  gratitude for all I am fortunate to have,
  to question whether I need all the other stuff.

I thank you, God, for Michelle.
  Bless her this night and all her nights.

SEARCHING FOR THE ABUNDANCE BORN OF POVERTY

I'm asked to write Abundance Born of Poverty.
  Yet still, I sit staring at this empty white page,
  feeling the empty, broken space in my heart,
  blind to the abundance in this, my poverty.

Is it because I take comfort in the losses of poverty?
  Is it because I desire the liberation of exoneration?
  Is it because I cannot see beyond my fear and rage?

Why can't I see the abundance that I know must be there?
  I really do want to trust Spirit's elusive and baffling gift.
  I really do believe I have been asked to give it voice.

Is my struggle to fathom abundance a part of the story?
  Perhaps, by giving voice to the doubt, I can affirm
  the doubt that clouds our hearts, and in so doing,
  open the way for Spirit to say,

'It's okay. I love you. I love you. I love you. I love you.
  I love you in your doubt, your suspicion, your disbelief.

There is no part of you that I do not love and treasure.
There is no part of you that I do not hold in my heart.'

So perhaps, this is a message in Abundance Born of Poverty.
My inability to believe is just one of many faces of poverty.
And, as I stand exposed by disbelief, I hear the declaration
of undying, unconditional love, abundance beyond measure.

FOR MICHELLE

My inspiration and my sister sat before me, sobbing.
Life has not been benevolent to her this last year.

We have held each other through this long drought,
laughing and crying together, assisting each other.

And, each day we awake with the resolve to step,
again and again, into the free-for-all that is life.

'Money doesn't really mean much to me,' she smiles.
'I don't want a lot. I just need a place to sleep.'

'I don't want alms. I want to be able to support myself.
I need the opportunity to make my business profitable.'

I gaze at her tired, beautiful eyes and see an aching soul,
exhausted from the brutality of living on the streets.

The never-ending struggle to survive encircles her
like a tourniquet, squeezing the chi from her lungs.

Fortune in life, I believe, is not accorded by merit.
It is a gift for which we are largely not responsible.

Claiming deservedness blinds one to the gift and
to the opportunity to know profound gratitude.

I pray that life's gifts will be lavished on my dear sister.
I pray that Spirit gifts all she needs to journey her path.

And, I pray that we remember that all gifts are blessings
for which the only apt response is profound gratitude.

Namaste, my dear Michelle.
I love you.

HANDS REACHING THROUGH THE DARK

'You will need to ask for help.'

Those words rose in my mind without warning.
  Another insult on this journey that seems
  destined to end in the demise of my ego.

'You will have to ask for help.'

The shame, the embarrassment,
  the disbelief, the shock, the shame,
  that for all my effort, I can't get it right,
  that I can't be the right person for the job,
  that I can't find a way to feed just one person.

That I am failing my children and my self,
  that I am superfluous to this economy,
  that I am extraneous and unwanted,
  that I disappoint my aunt and me.

All these emotions roll through me like ocean waves,
  drowning the calm, the peace, I work so to fashion,
  washing what little wisdom and faith I can muster
  out to sea, broiling, wind-blown, enraged, cold.

What is more devastating, I wonder,
  learning how to live in the next level of poverty, or
  learning how to live with the next level of self-hate?

'You will have to ask for help.'

Amidst this chaos, I journeyed to Silverton.
  I knew how fragile I felt, how hard it
  would be to maintain myself.
  Still, I journeyed there.

I told myself I just needed to laugh,
  to delight in the time with my friends.
  I held the ruse successfully the first day.

But, the struggle of it wore thin
  the facade I had hobbled together.
  And, the second day, it all unraveled.

'I'm too proud to ask. I'm too broke to eat.
  I'm too weak to bow and too strong to bleed.'

Over and over again, the women chanted the stanza,
  cutting deeply into the wound that was my heart,
  ripping through the tattered veneer, and baring
  my exhausted and shattered soul for all to see.

They sang, 'Can you sing words of comfort?
  Can you break through me, strong hands?
  Can you undo me enough to heal me?
  Take the weight from my shoulders.'

'You will have to ask for help.'

Exposed, I ran to hide my pain and shame,
  but they followed, paying no heed to the
  doors closed to my room and my heart.

They held me, loved me, prayed for me,
  cried for me...and would not let go.

'You will NOT be homeless', they said.
  'You are not alone. You are not alone.'
  Again and again, they repeated the words.

At first, I couldn't hear their words,
  because they were not meant for me,
  because I could not receive them,
  because I did not believe them,
  because I really am, all alone.

But, they wouldn't stop.
  Their presence and promise
  defied the reality I thought mine.

And suddenly, I understood the reason
  I journeyed to Silverton that weekend.
  I went to discover that I am not alone.

Broken heart, beyond self healing.
  Hands reaching through the dark
  to touch, to hold, to heal, to love.

Abundance Born of Poverty.

CASTING ASIDE THE 'OTHERS'

Yesterday I contemplated how essential it is for human beings to know they have something to offer in this life and to feel that the world values their contribution.

This need surpasses even the need for food and water. It ties people into the web of life on this material plane, catalyzes the synapses between people and the community of which they are a part.

Being valued is fundamental, essential, necessary for life.

So, when people's value is appropriated through intent or apathy, the breath of life is literally squeezed from them, leaving empty shells where once there lived a vibrant force of promise and hope.

Our economic system requires a 6% unemployment rate. Certain groups of people are sloughed off from the economy and relegated to this 6%. The groups include those who are aging and disabled, women and youth, African American and Hispanic. The list goes on.

Stripping the 6% of work renders them superfluous to the economy and deprives them the means to feed and clothe themselves. When they ask for help in the basics of living, the economic system disparages their existence and the drain they put on those 'who make an honest living'.

Their food stamps are cut. They are told to 'pull themselves up by their bootstraps', conveniently ignoring the fact that our economic system stole their boots! Then, stories are invented about how decrepit and deceitful they are.

In the stories, they are cast as the 'Other', people different than us, less valuable, morally reprehensible, not deserving, a sinkhole into which our hard-won earnings disappear. And, we are taught to believe the stories.

Of late, it's dawning on me that I have become one of the 6%. I am no longer merely witness and scribe. I am the 'Other'. I feel the crushing force of the brutal, heartless system that would steal my breath and deny my life force.

These words I speak are not a political argument or stance.
  This is about rising up and accepting our humanity,
  donning the amour of love and compassion,
  setting foot on the cold, hard realities
  that our economic system creates
  for so very many amongst us.

And, understanding this,
  it is about reaching
  our hands in love
  to all beings.

It is no less than that.

HEALTH AND HOMELESSNESS…NOT

As the cold morning air vitalizes my sleepy mind,
  my body shivers, recalling the warmth of my bed.
  Savoring hot coffee, I make a warm bowl of cereal.

My body rejoices in the waking up, food and warmth.
  And then I remember my dear friend who is homeless.
  She woke up to the dawn freeze in the back of her van.

She has no heat source to make warm coffee or breakfast.
  Her food stamps will not purchase warm, prepared food.
  So, cold and stiff from another night in her freezing van,
  she must choose, cold and uncooked food or junk-food.

Snuggling at home, I eat my cereal and sip on my mocha
  while my friend sits in a van in a fast-food parking lot
  eating a cholesterol-ridden, vitamin-deficient diet
  and drinking tepid, brackish water called coffee.

THIS IS WHERE I AM

I haven't been writing lately.
  It's not that words aren't asking for release.
  No, it's that I am focusing ALL my energy
  into transforming my vision into reality.

Sometimes in life, you have to
  focus your energy like a laser beam on your vision;
  align all your actions to be in service to that vision;
  block out everything else.

Sometimes in life,
  you have to run like hell toward the finish line,
  even when your legs ache and your vision blurs,
  and most significantly, when your heart falters.

You put your heart and soul into it.
  You give it everything you have.
  You give it your every breath.

Then you await the universe's response,
  practice breathing, and
  allow for miracles.

THE LIGHT AND THE PROMISE

So focused have I been on carrying out the plan.
  Each moment, I have dedicated to its fulfillment.
  Waking and asleep, my mind has been working it.

Yet, I heard Your call, once again, from my heart.
  Finally, after many months, I heeded your call,
  lit the candles and sat in silence to listen.

I was at the base of the great oak tree.
  She came to me, the White-Wolf-Woman.
  She took my hand in hers and raised me up.

We walked the earth and sky to the black universe.
  There, she let go my hand and showed me the portal.
  'It is yours, if you wish,' she said. 'The choice is yours.'

The light, alone in the black, drew me forward. I wanted it.
  I wanted release. I wanted peace. I wanted the grief to end.
  So, I moved eagerly toward it, anticipating another future.

Then I saw an elderly woman curled tightly on the ground,
  clad in rags, drenched from the rain, her life force fading.
  She reached feebly to touch the light and the beyond.

I can choose the light. I am so weary from this life.

Then, I realized I could embrace the woman
  warm her aching body, care for her heart.
  And, I could deliver her soul to the light.

So, I took her in my arms, held her gently,
  poured my love into her broken heart
  and my tears onto her lifeless face.

Then, I carried her to the portal,
  to the guardian angel, waiting
  with eternal peace and love.

As the woman disappeared,
  the angel looked to me,
  awaiting my decision.

How easy it would be to slip into light.
  How tempting the promise of peace,
  the release from the aching and fear.

Sensing my indecision, the angel passed
  the promise of pure love and peace
  from eternity into my wounded spirit.

And I realized,
  I cannot join those ready to step beyond.
  There is more for me to do, to live, to be.

There are so many in so much anguish,
  so many that cry for warmth and love,
  so many that have nothing and no one.

So, I chose to step back into life,
  armed with the promise inherited by all
  from a Grace beyond our comprehension.

IMAGINE, DARE, SOAR

Had a vision as I was writing yesterday.
  I was suspended in midair, arms outstretched.
  The air rushed past my body and through my hair.

Startled to suddenly find myself in this dilemma,
  I looked back in time to find this story's beginning.
  I saw myself running up a big hill, straight to the cliff.

When I reached the hilltop, I did not hesitate.
  No, I opened my arms and ran to the cliff's edge.
  My last step on Gaia was the first step of my launch.

I dove off that cliff, arms outstretched.
  And this is where I find myself,
  wind whirling all-round me,
  Gaia rushing to meet me.

I've been here before in this life.
  I have felt wings grow, the air lift me.
  I have seen myself fly through tempests.

But, never has my material well-being
  been so precarious, so lacking recourse.
  My rainy-day savings dry in the spring sun.

As I hurtle past my friends, they smile to me,
  'Something will work out. Everything will be fine.'
  I smile, 'Yes, something will happen and I will be fine.'

But, I know our words hold different meanings.
  They talk of jobs and security, food and shelter.
  I speak of my soul's purpose in this mortal frame.

Watching the earth rush toward me, I know that
  whatever ensues, I will not crash into the ground.
  Because you see, this is not the journey of a mortal.

It is the journey of a soul embodied in dirt-made-flesh.
  I do not control the wind or gravity or whatever comes.
  My body may smash into Gaia, but my soul will take flight.

So why, you ask, did I dive off the cliff in the first place?
  I dove because I had a vision and an opportunity to live it.
  I dove because it was mandatory to make this vision a reality.

So I am midair now, wind blinding me, Gaia fast approaching.
  My arms outstretched, my soul feeling peace and gratitude.
  I am living with everything I have, with every last breath.

Imagine, dare, soar

THE CRASH AND THE FLIGHT

and though my body may crash into the earth,
  my spirit will soar,

because nothing can clip the wings of God, and we...
  we are God incarnate.

When Things Get Dicey

The unimaginable is taking dramatic form.
  In my sleep, it splashes the canvas with fears
  that I will not allow to emerge in the light of day.

Startling, devastating and true are the images.
  Ancient heartaches, roused by the scent of fear,
  recast themselves as demons, claws set for the kill.

I awake in a fright, the unimaginable fused to
  my eyes so that wherever I look, there it looms.
  I am free-falling, headlong, into the unimaginable.

I AM Caring For You

Last night, I gave Spirit an ultimatum.
  'Gift me with my work!' I demanded.
  Or I will take life into my own hands!'

I trusted that the strength of my resolve
  shone through my words and demeanor.
  I hoped that Spirit paid heed to my appeal.

'I have designed a path forward,' I say.
  'I am walking that path. I will continue.'
  Yet, I worry Spirit does not desire this path.

A whisper, a friend, a stranger, a teacher.
  All tell me this is not the path I am to walk.
  It is a step en route to the path, a gift for me.

So, I fall to my knees in prayer,
  'Please Spirit, gift me with my work.
  I am wasting precious time, every day.'

I remember that a friend recently asked if my
  impending financial collapse is my greatest fear.
  My response was, 'No. That is not my greatest fear.'

My greatest fear is that I will not find a way
  to give back to life, to gift myself and my talents,
  to make this life a joy and a blessing for all, everyone.

I feel the press of time against my bones,
  and in the depths of my feminine physique.
  Time passes ever more quickly to my demise.

And yet, I wait.

I hear, over and again, that my reach for security is
    misdirected, is not how I am to use my energy.
    Rather, I am to follow my heart's yearning.

This morning, relinquishing my demand on Spirit,
    I tried to quiet my mind to receive wisdom and council.
    Despite my limited success at quieting myself, Spirit spoke.

Spirit said, 'Do not take a definite position.'
    'Refrain from criticizing the process
    that is occurring within you.'

'Wait...Within Me?' I asked, startled.

I hadn't considered the idea that these are not delays,
    but rather are essential elements of this Spirit-led
    process that is nurturing a ripening within me.

Spirit advised me to have faith, to relax into the flow,
    to gift myself with the freedom to allow the unfolding,
    to follow Spirit's call and trust Spirit to grant my security.

Moments later, I received a note from a friend
    to whom I owe a debt, releasing me from the debt.
    Amid tears of gratitude and astonishment, I heard Spirit,

'I AM caring for you. Face forward.'

RÉSISTANCE

The defeat of my plan is absolute.
    All the universe answers me as one, 'NO.'

No false hopes have been offered.
    Just the abiding and patient answer, 'NO.'

Messages to 'Let go. Stop pushing.'
    I counter them all with resolute résistance.

I had an epiphany with the first light.
    Spirit upturned my world with purpose.

Something different draws near.
    Concealed until my résistance collapses.

Hallelujah, Hallelujah, Hallelujah.

SUPPRESS THE WILL, ADDRESS THE SOUL

A depression is trying to settle in,
  fogging my brain,
  slowing my motion.

It wants me to lay down,
  stop thinking,
  stop trying to
  figure it all out.

Just be.
  Don't talk to anyone.
  Don't do my work.

Sleep, dream, be quiet.

Alone is best.
  A crowd is fine.
  Anonymity is safety.

Can't figure it out.
  Can't engage my brain.
  No jump starts.

Don't care.
  Don't want to figure it out.

Dull, quiet, resting.

Tears ever present,
  threaten to burst
  through the tightly held,
  but fragile veil.

To keep them at bay,
  don't interact.
  Just stay quiet.
  Don't think.
  Don't do.

Just rest and be.

My soul needs me,
  to depress my mind,
  suppress my will,
  address my soul.

WIND-UP HUMAN TOY

'So...just...let...go?! That's what you want?!' I cry.
  'You presume this request is an easy feat, Spirit!
  But it doesn't feel so easy to me. Not at all!'

'Why is the wisdom you share always a puzzle?' I demand.
  'Why can't you say it in simple-to-understand language
  rather than codes and images I am loath to examine?!'

'Perhaps, you laugh merrily at my solemn approach,
  my weary eyes, bewildered mind, and aching heart.'

'You turn the key on me, the wind-up-human toy,
  and watch as I march around in endless circles
  or simply just run out of steam and fall over.

'No matter,' say you. 'I can just wind her up again.'

'No matter,' say I. 'Nothing matters, really, does it?'

PAUSE

Dark, Angry

Is there anybody out there?
  Is there anybody in here?

No, just the black emptiness.

Floating in the void.
  Nice thing about voids,
  there is nothing there...

You laugh, but really.

My anger, my self-pity, my fear,
  the struggles, the trials, the errors,
  the time that so mercilessly slips away,
  the noise from endless battles against self,
  the cacophony of insanity called civilization.

All dissolves into nothingness in the void.

It is not such a bad place,
  at least for this moment.

I can interrupt the incessant struggle,
  discharge the scorching energy,
  inhale, finally, a full breath.

Pause.

ARE YOU READY? I AM WAITING.

OK, I have a confession.
  I have been really pissed of late.
  I got so pissed that I shut out Spirit.

I donned my worn and ragged coat-of-armor.
  This coat-of-armor is so much part of
   me that it has its own name,

'I will get through this myself...damn it!'

Funny I didn't feel the breeze
  through the many holes and tears
  in that age-old and thrice-mended coat.

I know that it really isn't a coat-of-armor.
  It's me hiding, pushing out my chest,
  believing it is up to me alone to
  get myself through this life.

The purpose - still - feels so right.
  'How,' I wonder, 'can wanting a job
  be a bad thing? Is it strange to want work
  that pays a living wage and medical coverage?'

Yet, all my efforts and education and experience
  bear no fruit. And now, my friends, I will share
  the truth behind why I haven't been writing.

I have been ashamed to admit that I am
  in this place, once again, after witnessing the
  wisdom that Spirit channels through my fingers.

I guess I hold hope that these gifts of Spirit
  would soak through my coat-of-armor
  and change forever my deficiencies.

But, I remind myself...it is a process,
  yes, a journey. And I am on the path.

The gifts of Spirit are still here, available
  for me when I am ready to receive them.

So, Spirit asks once again and forever,
  'Are you ready? I am waiting.'

STEP IN WHEN I FALL

Of my many failings, I doubt
  at day's end, I will be faulted for
  not having giving it everything I had.

The dents and bruises on my brow
  attest to my tenacious and sometimes
  obstinate endeavors to actualize my life.

And for one who endeavors so hard
  to blaze the trail, to find my way,
  to be a responsible co-creator...

The words, 'You're trying too hard.'
  are tantamount to, 'Do not be you.'

Gasping, desperately constructing my defense,
  proclaiming, 'But, it is my responsibility!'
  I'm supposed to take care of myself.
  I can find my way! I will do it!'

Caught in the whirlwind of my own making,
  I, the whirling dervish, spin and push and spin.
  Bleeding, I push harder with deeper commitment,
  blinded by fear and distress, until, inevitably, I crash.

For one can hold that energy for only so long.
  Then I find myself in that oh-so-familiar-space
  of a substance less all its vital organs and structures,
  amoebic, heaped into a corpus of misdirected intention.

Finally, I say, 'OK, I give. Perhaps, it's not for me to decide.
  Perhaps I need to hand it over, to let go, to allow Spirit.'

And, I hope that Spirit will take that invite quickly,
  for I am practiced at getting up from this place
  and pushing forward when I need to lie still.

FAITH

Great Spirit,
  if I were to re-open myself to you,
  what would you say to me?

In my fear, I stepped away from You.
  I thought to take control of my life,
  not trusting that Your hand moved.

So hard have I been fighting, pushing.
  Yet, here I stand, bloodied forehead,
  tears streaking the ink on my paper.

Faith, so very difficult
  at precisely the moment
  I most need it.

INTO THE FLOW

There is a natural flow to life, like
  a stream flowing down the mountain.

When I chance upon that stream,
  and step foot in its cool waters,
  I am one with all the universe.

Yet, when I find myself stranded on the shore,
  I discover the storyline I fashioned wherein I must
  transform solid into liquid, or simply, move the earth.

And, just a step away from this epic, ineffectual battle
  of warrior against life, flows the stream, gleaming,
  inviting, patient, supple, cool, fresh, life giving.

This morning, I awoke realizing
  that I have not moved the earth,
  yet the stream flows just at my feet.

Spirit asked me to dream the life I desire,
  to strive toward my vision, and learn
  to accept when I have run ashore.

I get this when my efforts come to no avail,
  when each breath brings no chi to my lungs,
  when I am exhausted before the dawn breaks.

The stream is flowing right next to me, always.
  When I tire of the mêlée, Spirit guides me
  back to the refreshing, life-giving waters.

THE WISE CRONE

I am amused by this self.
   53 years and so much seeking, witnessing, learning.
   Yet still, I tread old paths, the ones I know don't work.

And, I set foot upon them at exactly the moment that
   I am asked to reset my direction, alter my true north.
   Is this the human experience, or am I just very slow?

I see myself as an elder woman, the Crone, sitting in
   my rocking chair, its voice as creaky as my own,
   singing into the melting day.

Hearing a laugh or remembering a tear,
   I turn my head and glance over my shoulder.
   In the beyond, I see one of the many moments lived.

And, in the witnessing, I am at peace, contented, happy.

For I know that, despite the agony or exhilaration,
   I lived each moment in the fullest expression of me
   to the best of my ability, with everything that I had.

When I am challenged by life to take another uncertain step,
   I visualize this wise crone. She inspires me to search within
   to find who I am and courageously step into the unknown.

My gait is awkward and I get tangled in my best intentions,
   but the wise old crone smiles, saying, 'You are doing your
   best and look, life is not quite as serious as you imagine!'

LOOK ABOUT YOU

I sense there is something new and different waiting.
   I'm witnessing myself dance with this invitation.

Résistance, attachment to a certain sense of self,
   fearing the loss of my identity, of sustenance.

Yet, Spirit persists, patient with my struggle.
   'Look about you,' Spirit counsels, 'look!'

Then, I am endowed with eagle sight.
   I see the riches that envelop me.

I see that they are ever-present,
   especially when I cannot see.

Perhaps it is time to let go
   and step into the flow.

DISCOVERING TREASURE

My financial insolvency shifts position from
  an unthinkable reflection on the distant horizon
  to a real potential in sharp relief just outside my door.

Yet, I discovered a reservoir of resplendent abundance.
  This treasure comes not from a person or thing or event.
  No, I discovered this treasure in a place deep within myself.

Its riches include a profound and gentle peace,
  a feeling of exquisite and humble gratitude for it all,
  a certainty, a strength and a clarity that shine light on dark.

My heart swells, and I fall to my knees in thanks for the
  treasure that always was, that enriched my every moment,
  that Spirit shared with me even as I concealed it from myself.

THE TREASURE WITHIN

Dancing on the wind,
  practicing my pirouettes,
  I have a sudden epiphany.

The ground I saw approaching,
  the canvas painted with my demise,
  all of it was a creation of my own mind.

It could not be an picture of my future because
  my future does not yet exist, and I am not psychic.
  No, I realized, it was a magnificent painting by
  that gifted and accomplished artist, my fear.

Awakened from its frenzied nightmare,
  my fear slumped, once again, into
  my arms, sobbing, tired, worn.

And the treasure within that
  revealed the illusion
  smiled with love.

THE HOLY DARK

The dark is ubiquitous,
  everywhere, ever-present,
  pierced only occasionally by light.

The dark is the mystery.
  It is the hidden, the unknown.
  It is the veil that hides the secrets.

There is more dark than light.
  But dark is not wicked.
  It is not treacherous.

The light allows us to see with our eyes.
  The dark invites us to see with our souls.
  Our souls open our eyes to the universe.

The holy dark.
  The mystery inside ourselves.
  Close your eyes, witness the All.

GIFTS OF SPIRIT

Receiving messages from Spirit.

The first message is that I frequently get in my own way.
  I then watched an incident wherein I did stand in my way.
  I witnessed as the prattle in my mind morphed into turmoil.

And, I learned that when I confer the turmoil of my making
  with my thoughts, feelings and energy, I cloud my vision,
  close my mind and constrict my heart. I am in my way.

The second is that I need to reopen my throat chakra.
  I remember when my voice was bright and strong.
  And, I remember when my voice was silenced.

Now I stand, book in hand, fearful that it is not
  good enough or worthy of publication, but
  trusting that Spirit is asking me to speak.

So, enriched by these gifts of Spirit,
  I refocus my gaze to these new
  and as yet untold possibilities.

And, I take another step forth.

FULL CIRCLE, DEEPER MEANINGS

I just realized that Spirit has brought me full circle.
  So elegant is she in her workings with my soul.

For months, I have been immersed in a deep lesson,
  to release gracefully things that are not meant for me.

I have traveled to many corners of this lesson,
  examined its intricacies, met its many faces.

Recently, I started to understand, to recognize when
  something is not for me and to let go of it, gracefully.

And now, I am realizing yet a deeper meaning
  of this term, 'not meant for me'.

'Not meant for me' are those things or people that
  take me out of the flow, are not in my best interest.

'Not meant for me' is Spirit discerning, when I cannot,
  when something is life-giving and when it is life-taking.

'Not meant for me' is when Spirit advises me that some
  thing is life-taking, and then guides me back to the flow.

'Letting go, gracefully' is recognizing Spirit's call and
  trusting Spirit acts out of pure and absolute love.

'Letting go gracefully' is stepping into the flow,
  and if I cannot, allowing Spirit to carry me.

MY PRACTICE

My practice
    to set my attention on this moment,
    on what I can do right now, and
    to not let fear take hold of me.

I feel strong and up-to-the-challenge.

It is a worthy practice,
    to set your intention,
    to live in the present,
    to allow the future.

KRIYA

Kriya, that's the word for what happens
  to my body since the Kundalini emergence.

It rises through my crown chakra and
  sparkles around my head with epiphanies.

It puts pressure on my throat chakra
  when creation is stirring and wants form.

It burns in my root chakra,
  anticipating new growth or awakenings.

And sometimes, it captures my body
  in a storm of chaotic, exploding energy.

It happened again, quite unexpectedly,
  as my friend did reflexology on my feet.

Awakened once again, the energy sparked
  and danced through all the muscles of my body.

The energy cascaded from one twitching muscle to
  the next, inciting a riot of chaotic, uproarious potential.

I could feel each of the thousand muscles in my body,
  the individual explosions, the bed quaking under me.

I was happy that the Kundalini is still alive in me.
  I was fascinated by the work of Spirit in my body.

As the Kriya subsided, I fell into a profound peace.
  I felt at One with Spirit and fully alive in this body.

I was reassured that my work is not complete,
  and that Spirit is here, now, for us all, always.

NEVER FORGET

Each moment is a blessing,
  especially the difficult ones.

It is not about what we deserve.
  It is about what we are gifted.

Take pleasure, pass it on,
  and never forget!

It is all a gift.
  All of it.

No Greater Blessing

Yesterday, I cried,
  'If you have not need of me, please take me home!
  I see no reason for existence except to gift to life.
  Please! Don't leave me here without purpose!'

For, much as I fear my imminent financial collapse,
  I fear most that I offer nothing of value to Spirit.
  The possibility is unthinkable, preposterous to
  one who dedicates her all to gift back to life.

Through my tears, I felt Spirit's whisper in my heart.
  'Look. Today, you have an opportunity to give.'
  I have, today, a meeting with the food bank.
  So, wiping my tears, I started to prepare.

Later, I left the meeting deeply conscious that
  Spirit entrusted me with a precious task.
  I get to give back to life with my life!
  There is no greater blessing.

Gratitude

I have been gifted with a responsibility.
  It does not come with wages and benefits.
  More importantly, it offers manna for my soul.

Yesterday morning, my soul wept.
  I feared I had no reason, no purpose here.
  Today, my soul rejoices at my opportunity to give.

I cannot see beyond this moment.
  But, on this day, I am so deeply grateful.
  I am comfortable in the dark with my soul work.

WHISPERS

In the silence, a whisper.
  Then another,
  and another.

Whispers floating in space,
  peacefully meandering.
  No course, only being.

Whispers
  from the All
  that spoke existence.

Sensing only
  partial thoughts,
  unembedded feelings,
  disembodied consciousness.

Silence alive with whispers.
  Commotion verges on chaos.
  Possibilities dance into infinity.
  Future, past, now - all the same.

Creation in a whisper.
  Lives complete in one breath.
  Worlds born and passed with a sigh.

Stepping back from the mortal self.
  Quieting the mind to hear the silence.
  Becoming still to witness the All whisper.

HERE AND BACK, AGAIN

As I travel through this life,
  I bring the core elements of me.

Like a corkscrew, the core of me
  winds its way into various situations
  no matter where I am
  no matter what is happening.

The energy that is me
  flows up and down that corkscrew,
  lingering now in this moment
  and flowing once again into another.

There is only one way
  that the energy that is me
  will leave this corkscrew...
  through the top.

One day, I will be finished
  with the work I've come to complete,
  and my energy will move effortlessly
  up the corkscrew and gently
  flow out of the tip.

If you are watching,
  you'll see a spray of sparkles,
  dancing lightly before dissolving into the ether.

But, I won't be gone.
  I will be the pure energy
  from which I...and you...emerged.

And, I will be deciding
  the next journey
  on which to embark
  to unravel yet another
  lesson for this soul.

ABUNDANCE MINDSET

If we believe in abundance, we are in concert with nature.
For, nature is the embodiment and essence of abundance!
In fact, for nature to flourish, there must be abundance.

There must be abundance in diversity, or Requisite Variety.
As in nature, so to in society. People of all colors, races,
beliefs and cultures are required for survival of humanity.

There must also be abundance in likeness, or Redundancy.
We need people who have similar talents and gifts, and
who bequeath them in partnership for the benefit of all.

Love expands exponentially the more we love.
So too, the gifts we offer back to life multiply
the benefits received by all, including ourselves.

So, look for diversity in the people around you.
Look for the similarity in the people around you.
Celebrate and learn from the diversity and similarity.

With an abundance mindset, there is never too little.
Rather the reservoir of love and life from which we
can draw enlarges to infinity as we open fully to love.

WE WILL WALK

While at the movies with my grandson,
  I received a call from a man whom I
  shall get to know well, offering me a job.

I had been listening for that call all day,
  carrying my cellphone in my pocket,
  the ear bud crammed into my ear.

Hearing nothing, I turned my focus to Kai.
  My journey had taken me so far from him
  these last months, and our long-overdue
  Nanna/Baby date was finally underway!

So, hand-in-hand and loaded with chocolate,
  popcorn and delight, we entered the dark
  hall and settled into our adventure of
  good guys, bad guys, and fantasy.

At the movie's end, cradling my little
  sleeping angel in my arms, I warily
  turned on my cell and waited for
  the voicemail to sort and share.

Then, his voice barely audible,
  his intention unmistakable,
  my future opening...

Spirit delivers wonderful miracles
  with incredibly impeccable timing.

Little boy in arm, lights dimmed,
  credits rolling, music thundering
  the words 'We want you' playing,
  I cried.

The boy-angel wakened,
  looked around and asked,
  'Nanna, why are you squeezing me?

'Come back to center, little one,' smiled the Creator.

'My work for you is far from complete.
  We start now a new journey wherein
  you will create that for which I have
  prepared you all these many years.'

'Savor this moment. Rest and relax.
  Cradle my child in your arms.
  Catch your breath, heal.'

'For, we have work to do.
  We will walk together into
  the future I crafted for you.'

'You will bring glory to My name
  and rest to My people
  through all you do.'

'I will not let you forget.'

'I have given you the experience
  for the story I will draw
  from your fingertips.'

'Open yourself, trust Me.
  We will walk now.'

JUST ONE MOMENT

The day after I got word, I felt a toxic energetic sludge stir
  within my body, through every cell, festering, deadening.

I hadn't noticed it before, but, I was sure it didn't just appear
  on that day. No, it has been building all the past 18 months.

I have been working so hard to maintain my center, stay calm
  in the eye of the storm, pay attention, care for my body.

Yet still, it found its way in and settled, coiled, dormant,
  waiting for just one opportunity to grow into dis-ease.

I let myself fall into a healing space, cleansing myself,
  purging the venom, allowing Spirit to heal and renew.

And, I think, once again, of those less fortunate than me,
  who don't have healthy food, or a warm bed, or safety.

And, I know that their bodies and hearts cannot fight the
  omnipresent scourge of dis-ease.

So, those most vulnerable to life are also most vulnerable
  to sickness, pain and suffering piled atop grief and despair.

I weep, I pray, I beg for just one moment of peace
  for all those who suffer at the hand of life.

Just one moment, please.

ABUNDANCE BORN OF POVERTY

Had I known the journey for which I was fated
  when I accepted the calling, I may have retreated.
  It seems such an extreme means for my illumination.

Yet, Spirit felt I need live that which I will dare to speak.

I embarked on my new career just two weeks prior to
  closing my bank accounts and becoming homeless.
  My first paycheck arrived in time to pay my debts.

The timing of my rescue from financial collapse
  suggests nothing less than a grand miracle
  through the grace of a Divine presence.

Yet, to focus solely on this marvel
  would obscure the many gifts
  bestowed on the journey.

Looking back, I notice
  them everywhere,
  offering exactly
  what I needed
  at precisely
  the perfect
  moments.

Abundance Born of Poverty

2 LOVE BORN OF HATE

THE BIRTH OF LOVEWORTHY

As my journey into poverty was beginning,
  I was preparing my first book for publication.

In 'Spirit Walk: Journey of a Soul Embodied',
  I shared the story of coming out as a lesbian.

In a lament echoed by many branded 'Other',
  I entreated life, the world and myself.

'I am a child of Spirit, as are you all,' I wept.
  'Why am I hated, by you, by you, by me?'

As I sent the book off to publication,
  I realized the story was not yet finished.

From the wellspring of my coming out
  was born Loveworthy, a plea for love.

The story finds its way into this book
  for it reveals another face of poverty, hate.

And, it reveals abundance beyond measure, love.

TODAY, IN THE SHADOW OF LOVEWORTHY

The landscape, dreamlike, floated past her motionless body.
  Reliving the events recently past threw her into a vast,
  swirling pool of confusion, revelation and incredulity.

'Did this really happen?!' echoed through her mind.

The memories captured her,
  binding her body to the earth,
  opening her mind to the universe.

It started so innocently and gently.
  She saw Loveworthy, felt at once a
  connection, a profound love for her.

She followed eagerly the mystique.
  Loveworthy knew her immediately,
  and without pause, they united as one.

There are those you meet in this life
  with whom you share a soul-contract,
  a covenant to share a hallowed journey.

So, they loved and walked,
  fell deeply one into the other,
  shared exquisite bliss and delight.

Then, a man swaggered out from the mist,
  clad in grays and browns and garnished with
  eyes of steel and a smile contorted into a scowl.

He too knew Loveworthy,
  and approached her with the
  arrogance born of power and rank.

Sanction and consent, his to confer,
  he wasted not a breath pronouncing
  his opinions and judgment against her.

'What are you doing?!' he exclaimed.
  'Who do you think you are, parading
  around like this, with another woman?!'

Loveworthy spoke not, but gathered her
  partner's hand in hers and stood silently,
  resolutely defying his dogmatic judgment.

In revulsion, he disappeared back into the mist.
  The women gazed into each other's souls and
  vowed that nothing would separate them, ever.

But as they walked, more stepped from the mist,
  lambasting them with profanities surpassed only
  by the hatred and disgust coursing in their hearts.

Acerbic ridicule escalated into physical threats.
  Loveworthy stood fast, devoted to her partner.
  Peacefully, she asserted their right to share vows.

And as her community and family exiled her
  for this profound and singular love, she wept,
  her heart shattered by their hatred and betrayal.

Her heart grew hard with anger and defiance.
  She would never again kowtow to the doctrine
  of a community defined by ignorance, fear, hate.

She was inspired by the love of her partner
  to find and express the greatness in herself.
  They healed, developed and thrived together.

A love so precious could not be wrong,
  and she,
  she was love worthy.

So she and her partner stayed the course,
  created their lives and journeyed together,
  strengthened by their love and commitment.

But the others, fed by fear and ignorance,
  could not allow such a shameless display
  of love and pleasure between two women.

Nor could they abide deviation from dictums
  that bound tightly that community of believers.
  So, they set out to stop the abhorrent abomination.

Clandestinely, they approached Loveworthy's partner.
  'She is disgraceful. She can only mean trouble for you.
  Best you stop now, while you still can,' they admonished.

Frightened by the others, Loveworthy's partner drew to her.
  'I'm confused!' she cried. 'They say our love is not natural?!
  They call us immoral and wicked! Is our love worth this?'

The hate had poisoned her partner's heart and mind.
 It had made her question her own wisdom, and worse,
 made her doubt her own worthiness to be and feel love.

Loveworthy gazed at the one who made her heart sing,
 the woman with whom she shared a soul contract.
 And, she wept.

Brokenhearted, Loveworthy turned away.
 Their journey and their love had been
 desecrated by ignorance and fear.

They caught Loveworthy that day,
 walking alone by a stream.
 There, they took her.

She walks no more by the stream.
 Her light, her love, her life,
 all perished that day.

And here I lie, next to the stream,
 transfixed by the memories of the
 love that was mine and that I let go.

Through my tears, I see her spirit,
 I feel her touching my heart,
 and I realize, finally, that

 I am love worthy.

AN OLD WOMAN'S SCORN

'And did I tell you,' asked the old woman, 'there is no need for you to hang on to your hate for Loveworthy, or your contempt for her, or your anger at her?

'You see, there is no amount of hate or contempt or anger that you can direct toward her that she did not level in equal and greater measure toward herself. None!

'Hopefully, you are satisfied with that,' declared the old woman, eyes ablaze with mirth. 'Or do you need to exact yet more vengeance to heal your own wounds?!

'Tell me!' she shouted. 'What more could you possibly want?! What deep chord of discontent inside you was struck when Loveworthy learned who she was? And, why do you insist on targeting her as blameworthy for your own wounds?

'Do you really think this perpetual war against a broken woman will heal you? Does it satisfy some deep sickness in you to revel in her anguish?! When will it be enough?!'

Tears filled the lines that marbled her face. 'So old am I, and yet so astonished after all these years, to see the enmity that is humankind.

'I hoped, before I go, to witness the love that Loveworthy dreamed was possible. I wanted to take to my grave stories of human compassion such that the gods would smile.

'Yet, I have nothing for the passing except the dry bones of a long-dead child, whispers of dreams unfilled and dark contempt layered thick against my heart.

'And you,' the old woman asked, 'what have you?'

HATE

There is hate.

and

There is allowing hate.

It is all the same.

THE STORY WILL BE TOLD

'Damn you!' shouted Estelle quaking in her chair. 'How dare you steal the life from a young woman! Who the hell do you think you are, pronouncing judgment on the innocent and guileless who dare to love?!'

People had driven quite far to visit her, ostensibly to minister to the needs of an aged woman. But, they couldn't resist asking about Loveworthy. Guilt mingled with remorse, creating an amalgam of insatiable curiosity and morbid fascination. They needed to know, sought absolution for the sins of their fathers.

'You, with your cars and toys and rules! You know nothing of love! ' shouted Estelle. 'You know nothing of compassion. You know only your own fear and ignorance. Yes, ignorance!'

Swiping away the condescending hand of the preacher, Estelle warned, 'And, don't you dare tell me to quiet down! The gods will not smite me! I am older than most of them!'

Shaking violently, the old woman endeavored to quiet herself. 'Just what they would want,' she scoffed, 'for me to die right here so the truth won't be told! They can't kill me that easily!' She laughed and then chided herself, 'But Estelle, you will stop this old heart if you don't calm down!'

Smiling, she set again to the gentle rock that soothed her soul...and sometimes put her to sleep. She was, after all, near 100 and she deserved to sleep when she damn well pleased!

THE BIRTH OF A SOUL

'So, where was I?' Estelle snorted upon waking.

Rita smiled at the chutzpah of her dear friend. The people, mortified by Estelle's outburst, had driven back to their town. 'We were talking about Loveworthy,' she offered.

'Yes,' continued Thomasina. 'We agreed to tell her story. It's important because it is not just the story of one woman. It is the story of many who suffer at the hands of fear and ignorance feigned as authority and wisdom.'

'Right!' shouted Estelle, her anger freshly invigorated. And, somewhere, somehow it must end!'

'I never tire of talking about Loveworthy with you all. However Estelle,' Thomasina gently reproved, 'we need to tell the story to those who don't know it and need to hear it.'

Ever so slightly abashed, Estelle grew quiet. No one could speak to her like that except Thomasina. And Estelle knew she was right. She usually was.

Silence filled the room, disrupted only by the soft creaking of the rocker in motion. The women's eyes clouded with memories of a distant past.

'The community was overjoyed when they heard of Loveworthy's birth!' Estelle laughed.

'I remember that day like it was yesterday!' joined Rita. 'Like a princess, she entered this world...'

'all gooey, of course', interrupted Estelle. 'And, her cry filled the room near as powerful as the presence of her soul. Most didn't see her soul, but me, well I see these things.'

Noticing the dubious looks of her friends, Estelle retorted, 'Never mind you! I just do!'

'Her father was one of my favorite human beings' recalled Hazel, deftly changing the subject. 'He was a gentle soul, wearing the simple garb of a country pastor. "My princess" were the first words out of his mouth...that is, when he was finally able to speak!'

'And her mother, what an angel!' started Thomasina.

Laughing, Estelle interrupted. 'Any woman who could push out a screaming baby and then take it to her breast is crown royalty in my book!'

'I was outside the room,' continued Thomasina. 'There was such a commotion! The women were running to the phones to get word out to the congregation. The Pastor's family had grown by one beautiful girl!'

'Me and the girl's spirit watched all the hullabaloo for awhile,' said Estelle, eyeing her friends lest they mock her. 'Then, she said she had to go. She had a life to start.'

'So was born Loveworthy that summer day,' Hazel smiled.

'She was the apple in her father's eye!' Estelle continued. 'Could do no wrong, that one. Course, her father wasn't home during the day when she stripped off the dresses that her momma sewed to put on jeans and t-shirts.'

'She told her mother jeans were better to climb trees with,' recalled Hazel.

'And she was dead right! exclaimed Estelle. 'I swear that girl had more cuts and bruises than her brothers, part cuz she was always trying to keep up with them, and part cuz she believed there wasn't a tree she couldn't climb. Worried her momma sick, that girl.'

THE BELLE OF THE CHURCH

'Claire, you remember that Rita, Hazel, Estelle and I all lived in the same town as Loveworthy,' explained Thomasina.

'It was a really small town way out in the hinterlands' recalled Estelle.

Rita laughed, 'I still can't believe we all escaped! It was like living in a Twilight Zone movie!'

'I can't even imagine!' laughed Claire, a California native.

'Yes,' smiled Thomasina. 'It was so far off, word of events occurring in the outside world often arrived years after the events passed.'

'Yeah,' Rita smiled mischievously at Claire. 'You were smoking those special cigarettes in California long before MaryJane found her way to our town! Loveworthy used to joke that her brothers introduced the 1960s to the town's teenagers during the 1970s.' Claire laughed, 'those were high times!'

'Residents didn't pay heed to the workings of the outside world though,' said Hazel, uncomfortable with the MaryJane subject. 'There were crops to sow and cattle to milk.'

'Her parents being the Pastor and Pastor's wife, were celebrities in the town,' started Thomasina, redirecting the conversation. 'The folk in the congregation were deeply religious. And, they looked to Loveworthy's father for sage advice on all manner of things.'

'Right,' affirmed Rita. 'And, her mother was the grande dame of the town, leading the women's groups, playing the organ for the church choir, and baking for Sunday potlucks.'

'But, Loveworthy,' recalled Estelle, 'well, she escaped all the adult hullaballoo as quickly as she could and retreated to her favorite hiding places deep in the hollows of the church. I couldn't tell ya for certain where they was cuz I was old, even back then! But, she told me stories of her adventures.'

'The church was her second home, and she knew all the people. They were family, like aunts and uncles and cousins,' whispered Hazel, tears welling in her eyes.

'You have a lot of them when you are the Pastor's daughter...nearly everyone in town,' affirmed Thomasina.

'Which is why I just don't understand,' insisted Estelle, feeling once again the anger course through her veins, 'how her family could turn on her like that?!'

'It makes no sense,' offered Claire.

'No sense at all,' sighed Thomasina.

ONE THOUSAND 'YESES'

It was a quiet afternoon, like so many other Tuesdays. The women were quietly moving about their business. Estelle was fast asleep on her rocker, muttering and occasionally snorting. Hazel was working on her patches for the church women's quilt group. Thomasina was out back, working in the flower bed. And Claire had gone for a 'cigarette' walk at the park.

Rita enjoyed these times alone. This day, she was sifting through poems written by Loveworthy. She held one of her favorite, a tear glistening on her cheek. Loveworthy knew Rita better than anyone. Rita never understood how Loveworthy could see so deeply into her, how she could dredge her secrets from the dark caverns in which she had hidden them so long ago. Yet, she did, and she saw.

Loveworthy never told anyone Rita's secret. But she begged Rita to at least tell her friends, told her it was safe to come out to them. Rita never could. The danger was too high, the potential consequences too dire. No, she couldn't risk presenting her real self to the world. Instead, she spent her life being what other people wanted, all 86 years.

So, Loveworthy wrote her a poem, 'One Thousand Yeses'.
Tears glistening in her eyes, she read the poem yet again,
determined that this day she would tell her friends. Yes.

One Thousand Yeses
by Loveworthy, for My Friend

I said 'Yes', didn't I?
  How many times have I said 'Yes'?
  Time and again for so long, I no longer count.
  But, why?

Is there some magic number of 'Yeses' that,
  if said, cleanse the unworthiness that is me?

Can 'Yeses' clean the unclean,
  create desire for one unwanted,
  transform nothing to something,
  anything?

Or are they just desperate appeals
  to merciless spectators
  for acceptance,
  for love?

I can be no other than I am.
  I twisted and contorted myself
  for you and you and you, until
  there was left only a shell
  and a memory of love.

And still, after
  one thousand 'Yeses',
  I am not welcome,
  I am not loved,
  I am tolerated.

All because I cannot be
  who you need me to be.

So, I have one final 'Yes'
  That is to me.

I welcome myself.
  I love myself,
  because I AM.

Yes.

THREE THINGS IN LIFE

The women were gathered around their morning coffee when Hazel returned from church. She loved them all dearly, but wished they would join her on Sundays.

'I was thinking,' Hazel started.

'Oh no, not another rundown of today's sermon,' exclaimed Rita. 'I was just settling into the Sunday comics!'

'It would do you well to hear the word of God, for once!' Hazel retorted. 'But I'll spare you the teachings from today. I actually was thinking about Loveworthy.'

At mention of Loveworthy, all fell silent.

'I was remembering how her father worked such long hours, many times deep into the night. Loveworthy's mom told me how after she tucked her in for the night, Loveworthy would wait in the dark for her father to come home.'

'He always went to her room, no matter how late. Then they would have long conversations, exploring faith and philosophy and life and the universe.'

Thomasina smiled, 'Loveworthy told me that she treasured those moments above all others. All day, she would save her questions about life to share with him. He was her first hero...' 'and she was his princess,' finished Hazel.

Rita laughed, 'Loveworthy figured out early on about people who preached good stuff and then did bad stuff when others weren't looking. She would comment how those people acted like they were better than everyone else, but weren't. Like the preacher from the congregation across town. He would preach all about love on Sunday, but then treat his family dreadfully. Loveworthy saw right through that! She called him a fake. And, she was right!'

Taming the rising acrimony, Thomasina added, 'She also figured out the difference between knowledge and wisdom. I think all those nights talking with her father taught her that.'

Hazel continued, 'She wanted three things in life, to be one with her God, to be a good person, and to grow wise like her father. So she set about searching for wisdom. She turned to the greatest source of wisdom she knew, the Bible. She read it faithfully every night, talked with her father about it, attended Sunday School classes, listened as best a kid can to the sermons on Sunday, and then read the Bible some more.'

'I remember when she got to be 12-years-old,' chimed in Estelle. 'Her daddy and momma gave her a special Bible. It was written for teenagers. It was a proud day for Loveworthy as she was nigh on being a grownup teenager! And now, she had a Bible that spoke cool teenage language, not that strange language all the old people spoke.'

'She poured over that Bible,' said Thomasina, 'seeking wisdom, absorbing the words, shaping herself to fit the ideas, forming her thoughts to match. It was her quest. It was her life. She believed everything she read in that Bible.'

'It is, after all,' defended Hazel, 'the Word of God. How could there ever be anything better than the Word of God to learn wisdom?'

'Unless, of course,' offered the skeptical Rita, 'the Bible was incorrectly translated, or was an interpretation, not a direct translation.'

Hazel glared. 'I'm just saying,' defended Rita.

'Anyhow,' finished Estelle, 'she believed she had it from the Source. And, she stuck to it like glue.'

LIVING ON AND BORN AGAIN

The soft patter of spring rain beat in tune with the rocker. The intoxicating scent of spring flowers mixed in abundance with the fresh greens emerging from the sparkling mist hugging the ground. Scattered rays of warmth shone from the sun, teasing like a lover who just might give more...

This is the magic of living in the rainy country. Life piles up on itself. No sooner than a tree starts to decay, another sprout takes root in the nutritious rot and grows tall and proud, until it too succumbs to the master of time and gives itself over to yet another.

Could it be that the people of this valley, too, follow this natural rhythm? Not long gone, yet already providing the fodder for another's growth. And some, long gone, still offering the nourishment for those to come.

These are the thoughts that wandered through the old woman's mind as she watched time pass. Her furrowed brow wrinkled even more as a broad smile washed across her face.

'Loveworthy was like that,' Estelle thought. 'She's gone so long now, and still she reaches out. Her life can nourish others, if her story be told. That's why I hang on, to tell that story. Then, I can go, when I know someone heard it.'

So, wait she did for the people to come back. And eventually, they did. For something about Loveworthy caught in their throat, caused their heart to skip a beat. They wanted to know. So, they came.

'Some of you folks is those born-again types' started Estelle, peering into the crowd. 'I seen you at the tent the other day, heard the talk about the day someone was born again. I don't know bout that, see. I figure you was born once and that's just about enough. But, when I saw y'all out there, I remembered a story about Loveworthy.'

'Now, Loveworthy's parents didn't raise her in that born again religion. They was just regular Lutherans. I think they believe you're just born once too, but don't quote me on that. Better ask one of them Pastors.'

'Anyway, one day Loveworthy was late comin to my house. When she finally got there, she had this faraway look in her eyes. I seen this a bunch of times with her. She always seemed to be living here and someplace far distant at the same time. But this day was different.'

'This day she had tears in her eyes. "What," I asked her "got into you, child?" The day couldn't be any brighter and I knew she was building a tree fort that day. "Why the long face?" I asked.'

'As if pulling herself from a distant star, Loveworthy tried to focus on me. With tears in her bright blue eyes, she told me, "Last night when I was waiting for my dad, I felt Jesus come into my heart."'

'But child,' I challenged, 'you always feel close to
Jesus. It's near all you speak about, and that Bible of yours.'

"No!" she cried. "It's different! I actually felt him next to
me and then become one with me, in my body! I can't even
describe how it felt! I've been thinking and the closest I can
come is the time I jumped out of the tree into the leaf pile. It
felt like I was flying, like I could go anywhere I wanted with
just a thought, like I didn't have to pay attention to gravity,
like I could soar to the stars! That's how it felt!'"

'I was taken aback by that, didn't know how to
respond. Was her wild imagination taking her on another
ride? Was she slippin over the edge? I couldn't rightly
tell. But now that I think about it, it might nota mattered
what I said cuz soon as she finished telling me, she was far
away again.'

'She changed that day. She was always deeply faithful, like
her daddy. But, I think she really did see Jesus that night.
After that is when she started talking about being a missionary
in Africa, about dedicating her life to God.'

'And see, that's what she did. She protected the boy that
was slow-in-the-head from the bullies. She sang at the nursing
home on Sundays. She fought to save the earth. That's what
she did. Many a one was touched by that loving heart, some
of your parents too, I venture to guess.'

'So, you see. This is what I don't understand. And, maybe
you religious folks can explain it to me in simple language,
language even an old woman like me can understand.'

'How is it possible that this girl who gave herself entirely
to her God could be bad? How does someone with such a
tender, loving heart suddenly change with the tide of
hormones into the loathsome creature you all cast her to be?'

'Help me understand, cuz try as I might, I just don't get it.'

INNOCENCE

'That was the thing about Loveworthy,' said Rita. 'She never lost her innocence. She looked upon life as a child, full of wonder and curiosity and reverence. She could feel the sacred, always. Sacred was not a thing she did on Sunday. It was a part of her walk, how she perceived the world, how she dealt with life. To her, all of life was all sacred.'

'Me. I'm not so lucky,' said Estelle. 'I been through a lot in my years, seen a lot that I didn't want to see, you know? It put a hard coat on my heart. Now, it feels so crusty and thick I can hardly feel the beat of my own heart.'

'This all makes me wonder,' pondered Thomasina. 'What is this thing innocence? Is it a thing that you only get once in life, before anything bad ever happens to you? Is it fated to be a mere memory of a distant past? And, if that's true, how could Loveworthy hold it so long?'

'So, what is innocence?' Rita pondered.

'Well' started Hazel, 'It's my grandson. He's innocent.'

'Yes' joined Thomasina. 'My grandchildren are innocent too. But, do you know any adults who are innocent?'

That stopped everyone. 'Course, we thought of Loveworthy,' said Estelle, 'but who else?'

Silence filled the room as the women sorted through all the people in their lives. Coming up empty handed, Thomasina suggested a different approach. 'Perhaps, we aren't remembering the definition of innocence.'

Hazel, the book nerd, dug out her dictionary and looked up the word. 'Innocent...not guilty of a crime or offense,' she offered.

'No, Hazel.' claimed Rita. 'We're not talking about that kind of innocence. We all have that kind of innocence, except Claire, of course.' To that, Claire laughed and started rolling another of those special cigarettes she so loved.

'Yeah,' Claire added. 'Give us a different definition.'

'OK, give me a minute,' said Hazel, consulting her dictionary.

'Uncorrupted,' said she. 'Pure and uncorrupted by evil, sin, or experience of the world.'

Looking knowingly at Thomasina, Rita smiled, 'You remember that time in the tree house with Shawn?!' With Thomasina blushing, Rita continued, 'We've all had our tree house experiences. That definition rules out everyone but the priests...well, maybe! Try again, Hazel. What else does it say?'

'Naive....more trusting or guileless than most people through lack of life experience or failure to recognize the motives of others,' continued Hazel. 'Ignorant of something...having very little or no knowledge of something,' she finished.

The women sat silently for a moment, pondering the definitions, comparing them to their own lives, holding them as a flame to evaluate the lives of others they had known. The silence lingered on and with it, a sense of dejection settled in.

'How could it be,' asked Estelle, 'that among all us old women we can't find anyone aside from Loveworthy that matched those definitions?'

Finally, Thomasina started. 'It seems to me that innocence is something you are destined to lose. You are born with it and it dies as soon as you experience life. Some are lucky to keep their innocence longer, but others lose it just as soon as they enter this life.'

'That's right,' agreed Hazel. 'Just think how vulnerable you'd be if you didn't learn about the perils in life. Ignorance is dangerous. You have to know about hot stoves and dangerous men and dark alleys or you just won't survive!'

Inhaling from her cigarette, Claire considered her friends. Estelle loved the smell of those cigarettes. One time, Claire convinced her to try one. She never laughed so hard in her life, 'cept that is,' she remembered, 'till the next time she offered me one! But, that's another story,' Estelle smiled.

Estelle emerged from her reverie as Claire was talking. Her words weighed heavily on the hearts of all the women.

'How,' Claire asked, 'can it be possible that we were all destined to lose innocence? The animals keep it. The children are born with it. We were all children one time. It feels like a death to me. I don't like that! Maybe, we just haven't figured it out yet. Don't you all want it? Can we even remember how it felt?'

At that, a light glinted in each woman's eyes as she reached far back to capture the faded memories, to feel again the innocence that once was hers. They sat quietly for a long time, reaching back, remembering, and smiling.

'I remember...' started Claire Voyyd.

ALLOW THE POSSIBLE

'You all know I grew up in Southern California,' said Claire. 'I was the classic California Girl. At least I tried to be anyway. And believe it or not, I had a figure to die for!'

'We had another bonfire party going. The booze was flowing and a fog of MaryJane billowed all round us. I don't know what it was that night. But, something felt different.'

'I was just settling into the party when suddenly the voices and music were silenced. It was really trippy! I could see my friends' lips moving, but couldn't hear their voices?! I knew the radio was still playing because kids were dancing on the beach and I could see them laughing, but I couldn't hear any of it?! It was the strangest thing...' A perplexed expression washed over Claire's face as the memory surfaced.

'Then, I realized I could hear the ocean and the wind. It was a gentle night, just a slight breeze. I could hear the waves lapping against the shore! And, I could hear the wind blowing through the trees on the dunes.'

'My friend elbowed me. Apparently, she had been saying something to me, but I hadn't heard. Now, she was yelling at me. I knew that exacerbated look. But, I couldn't hear her. Any other time, this would have totally freaked me out. But, I was fascinated.'

Claire emerged from her reverie long enough to see the grins on the women's faces. 'No!' she snapped defensively. 'I wasn't stoned! Geeze! Give me a break! It's not like I was always stoned!' Rattled by Claire's rebuke, the women sank into their chairs, tight lipped and stone-faced.

She took a deep breath, and then a long, slow drag from her cigarette. No one moved. 'Anyway, I left the bonfire. It was the wrong energy. Even though I couldn't hear it, the noise really bothered me. I needed to be away from all of it. I needed to hear the waves. So, I left the party and followed the call of the ocean.'

'The closer I got to the ocean, the louder and more insistent its call became. Its pull was resolute, rhythmic and steady. I walked along the shore, listening, watching the waves in the moonlight, and feeling like I was finally where I was supposed to be. Nothing else mattered.'

'The moon light shone on the water in front of me. That sparkling, dancing patch of light shifted with every step I took. It drifted away, calling me, but wouldn't allow me to close the gap. I don't know how far I followed that light.

'Suddenly, Mark was next to me. I felt his arm slide around my waist, his hand touch my bare stomach.' Claire's face reddened as she recalled the moment. 'It, no he, was an insult to the sacredness of that moment!' Tightening her fist, she declared, 'It was all I could do to not belt him right then and there! How could he be so arrogant and presumptuous?!'

'I cut off his dim-witted come-on before he could get it out of his mouth and threw his arm off me!' Smiling contentedly, Claire continued, 'I told him to get the hell away from me...in no uncertain terms!'

The women giggled at this. They loved Claire's audacious and confident nature. They wished they could be more like her. They had grown reliant on hearing her stories, for through them the women could live for just a moment as beautiful, outspoken, carefree girls...and never have to step outside their tightly-bound comfort zones.

'The moon-on-the-water lingered, waiting for me to chase away that rude intrusion into our space. When I looked back, it was still there, whispering to me in the rhythmic pulse of the waves-on-sand. 'Relax,' it said. 'Breathe, feel the flow, be one with the flow.'

Claire's voice drifted off as if carried by the sea, tranquil and quiet. 'And again, I was walking. The waves lapped at my feet. The water was warm, inviting, luring.' The women watched in a hush, barely breathing, feeling the sand beneath their toes, captivated by the light.

'The next thing I remember,' whispered Claire, 'I was swimming along the shore, following the moon. The water caressed my skin as I rose and fell with the undulating sea. No longer was I Claire. I was not even human.'

Breathlessly she continued, 'I was the swell of the waves, the salt in the air. I was every droplet of moist, warm water washing over the land, supple, lush and full, divine and succulent. I was the sea.'

Mouths agape, the women stared into the vision, feeling alive in ways they had long since forgotten, desiring more...

Eyes closed, breathing deeply to center herself, 'OhhhKayyy then,' started Thomasina. 'That's an incredible story, Claire.' Pausing, 'but, I'm having a hard time seeing how it relates to the topic of innocence.'

'I don't know,' laughed Rita. 'But I'm feeling like I need to go off and finish this in private!'

'Rita!' gasped Hazel. 'I swear, you can take the sweet out of chocolate!'

'What?!' retorted Rita. 'Claire shared the chocolate! I'm just savoring it!'

'I'm sorry! But I just don't see how sexual escapades have anything to do with innocence!' objected Hazel.

'My dear Hazel. You really have to live a little before your tired old body can no longer rise to the challenge!' Rita mocked, laughing.

'hmmph...,' sighed Hazel, rolling her eyes in exasperation.

'Hazel,' Estelle chided, 'You know better than to challenge Rita! She gets your goat every time!' Rita smiled smugly.

'Well, I don't get it!' insisted Hazel. 'Will someone please tell me what sex has to do with innocence!?'

'I've been thinking,' stated Thomasina, unruffled by the exchange. 'Sex does have to do with innocence.' Pausing to reconsider... 'Yes, it absolutely does.'

'What?!' asked Hazel and Rita in concert.

'Well, think of it this way. We were all born sexual beings.' she started.

'Cept Hazel,' goaded Rita.

'It's part of who we are,' continued Thomasina, ignoring Rita. 'It's our physical make up. I know sex can be used to hurt people,' she continued, glancing at Estelle. 'But, in itself, and between people who love each other, it is beautiful.'

'You don't have to love someone for sex to be beautiful,' challenged Rita. 'God knows there'd be a lot fewer divorces if people could just get some without having to make all kinds of promises!'

'Rita,' scowled Estelle.

'No, I mean it,' claimed Rita. 'I've had plenty of experiences when we didn't play that game. We were just horny. Oh, sorry Hazel. We were aroused. Is that better?' she asked with a wicked grin.

'That's not what I was taught!' retorted Hazel, growing ever more uncomfortable with the exchange, but unable to stop herself.

'But, you don't get it, Hazel,' explained Rita. 'Just because we didn't love each other didn't mean we were perverts. We had physical needs and we were attracted to each other. We had some fun and then moved on. I'm still friends with some of those guys.'

'Yeah, I've had a couple of those experiences,' Thomasina reflected. 'The sexual act was beautiful, but only when we both respected each other. Hmmm,' she continued. 'So, are we saying that sex can be an expression of innocence?'

Estelle turned to Claire. 'Claire,' she said.

Claire's eyes reflected the sea, her cigarette smoldered in her hand.

'Claire...' spoke Estelle again.

Jolted from the dark wet, Claire struggled to refocus in the present. 'Yes?'

'Claire,' said Thomasina, gently. 'Can you tell us how your story relates to innocence?'

'That wasn't the end of my story,' whispered Claire, eyes turning inward again.

'Eww!' started Rita, grinning mischievously, to which Estelle threw up her hand. Rita sat back, knowing better than to push Estelle.

'I was swimming,' offered Claire after a moment. 'It was dark except that patch of moonlight on the water. I was following it, thinking that if I swam far enough I could finally catch it.'

'It was so quiet out there. The birds were asleep. No one was out there except me. All I could hear was the splash of my arms against the waves. For a while, I practiced swimming without creating any sound.'

'But then, I heard a big splash. It broke me out of the trance. You know you're in trouble in southern California when you hear a sound like that! I have friends missing arms...'

The women gasped as one, 'Ohmygod!' gulped Estelle.

'So, I froze, partly because I thought that's what I was supposed to do, but mostly because I couldn't move. I literally couldn't move! And, I couldn't get my brain to work. I was starting to freak!'

'In the moonlight, I saw it touch the surface of the water. It was swimming circles around me! It was then that I had one of those moments you've heard about, you know, when you see your entire life in two seconds? I was sure I was going to die, and I couldn't do anything to stop it!'

Claire paused. The women held their breath, frozen in the moment.

'Then, it turned and started swimming directly toward me. I was trying desperately to get my arms to move, to clench a fist. I thought if I was going to die, I was going to go out fighting. I would punch that damn shark right in the snout!'

'But I couldn't move. And, it was getting closer.'

'Suddenly, I felt a spirit surround me. I recognized it as the same spirit that had lured me into the water. It was the light on the waves. And then, I felt a sense of peace that I can't even start to describe. You know the one described in the Bible, the peace that passes understanding?'

The women nodded as one.

'Well, that's what it felt like, anyway.'

'And as that peace surrounded me, it melted the freeze that had captured my body. I could move again.'

'The shark was getting closer, but I no longer wanted to hit it. I just waited, feeling total peace and quiet.'

'At the last moment, I closed my eyes. I could see the moon-on-the-water inside my mind. I felt the wake from the approaching shark and heard his fin gliding through the water.'

'I waited...'

'A moment later, it brushed against me. It was sleek and smooth and cold. I opened my eyes just as it turned its head.'

'We stared into each other's eyes. It smiled at me. Then, it gently nudged its head under my arms. And, I finally realized. It wasn't a shark. It was a dolphin. It was holding me up in the water, making gentle sounds as if to say, 'It's okay.''

'I held on to its fin, and feeling my grasp, it slowly started swimming, carrying me along in its wake.'

'It was the most incredible thing. I felt like I was flying, but I was in the water! I was in the stars, gliding through the Milky Way, sliding down the rings of Saturn, perched on the North Star...'

'The dolphin brought me to a landing and after watching me climb to shore, it smiled again, that dazzling smile, and then swam away.'

After a long, enraptured silence, Thomasina spoke, 'Innocence...'

'Yes,' whispered Claire. 'Innocence.'

'Totally giving yourself over to life, right?' posed Rita.

'Allowing the possible to unfold,' ventured Hazel.

'Letting go of old ideas,' shared Estelle, 'so you can see things fresh.'

'Can we recapture that?' pondered Thomasina. 'After so many years? After all the heartaches and the sharks that really did bite?'

'I guess that's the question,' stated Estelle. 'Can we remember and bring back our own innocence?'

'And one more question,' offered Thomasina. 'Assuming we want to find our innocence again, how would it benefit us now, having most of our lives behind us and feeling more vulnerable than ever?'

LIFE IS SACRED

'I was thinking,' started Thomasina, 'about that time in the forest. Loveworthy loved the forest. Loveworthy yearned for the cold morning air tinged with the lush scent of pine, the towering trees pointing humbly to the magnificence that was the Rocky Mountains.'

'She believed that to be in the forest, she needed only the bare minimum of things from the human world. "Survival camping" she called it. She was always trying to figure out the bare essentials necessary to survive in the woods.'

'So, with a backpack filled with the bare essentials, she took to the forest. She would return from these ventures filled with stories of wonder, bears, eagles, trails that led to nowhere, sleeping under the stars and drinking from fresh mountain streams.'

'One day, filled with the magic of the forest, Loveworthy asked me to go with her. We drove into the country. It was so beautiful. Loveworthy turned onto a back road and we descended into a deep valley. Round the corner, we came upon a herd of cattle in the road. Finally, I had a chance to show Loveworthy my skills! You know, I grew up on a farm.'

'She parked the car, and we walked among the cows. I showed her how to call to them, to move them off the road. Oh, how we laughed! Cows going this way and that! Cows looking at us and wondering just what it was we wanted! Cows just standing there, chewing their cud, not at all interested in moving! Finally, we made a small path through the herd and drove through it to the wondering eyes of all.'

'Laughing, we drove on, deeper and deeper into the valley till the forest stood before us, inviting and dark. Without pause, Loveworthy drove into the woods, rolled down the windows and breathed as deeply as she could. The pine scent was intoxicating. The dark enveloped us and taught our eyes to see. The occasional bird call pierced the silence. The breeze, weaving its way through the trees, gently rocked the stillness. It felt as if we had entered a space so sacred, so magnificent, that the only appropriate response was to fall to my knees in prayer.'

'And, that's what Loveworthy did. She stopped the car and without a word, stepped into the quiet, so full of reverence that it radiated white around her. She stood quietly for a moment, her presence blending into the trees. Then, she fell to her knees and bowed her head to the ground. For several minutes, she kneeled there. The only sounds were the breeze through the trees and the beat of my heart.'

'Then she stood to face the east and raised her arms to the sky. In the silence, she reached to the heavens. I saw white light flow from the sky into her outstretched arms. She gathered the light in her hands and brought it down into her body, then held it near her heart. It washed through her and then gathered in her hands.'

'Holding her hands in front of her heart, she opened them to the woods and the light flowed from her to all in her path. The light filled the woods, sparkling off the leaves, dancing among the trees, and flowing deep into the woodland.

'Then, she turned to face the south and once again stretched her arms to the sky. The light fell from the sky and flooded her body. She glowed. And again, she opened her arms to the south letting the light shine to all in her path. She turned twice more, first to the west and finally to the north, gathering the light from above, using it to heal and cleanse herself and then sending it out to all.'

'Facing east again, Loveworthy brought her hands up into a prayer and touched first her forehead, then her chin and finally just above her nose. Each pose, she held momentarily. Though she uttered no words, I could hear the prayer of thanks given by each move of her body.'

'This prayer, she repeated in the other three directions until she finally came to rest facing north. I felt a tingling and saw that my skin was covered with goose bumps. As I looked into the forest, I saw the air alive with energy, a shimmer of white dancing atop the forest floor. And the stillness was as nothing I had ever before experienced. In that moment, I knew the 'peace that passes understanding'. I felt the universe in my soul. I was One with everything.'

'We didn't talk for a while after that. There were no words. But as we drove, I saw God in everything, in the flight of the eagle, the rush of the rivers, the sweeping of the pines in the wind, the laugher of a chipmunk...'

'That day, Loveworthy reminded me that life is a gift. We are part of that gift. We can let that gift flow through us to heal ourselves and then send it out to others in love.'

Life is sacred.

BITTER SWEET

'That was the other day!' shouted Estelle. 'It's no matter
to me today!' Turning, she stomped off.

'To where? To where am I stomping?!' she chided herself.
'I can't stop now! Have to keep going or they're gonna pester
me some more!' Stomping, slamming a door for good
measure. 'Okay, guess I don't have a choice. Have to go to
my bedroom again. Damn it!'

'For once, I'd just like to sit in the living room without
them forever nagging me to open up and talk! I open up
every day, don't I? I say "hi". I say "thank you". What more
could they want?!'

She slammed her door again to make sure they didn't dare
follow, and sat heavily on her twin bed. 'Now what?' she
wondered. 'Suppose I could read that magazine. Trouble is,'
she thought looking at the 1999 date, 'it's a bit old.'

'Oh well, nothing else to do.' So, she gathered up the
magazine, found her rocker and wrapped her shawl around
her shoulders. It was going to be another long day, and at
some point she was going to have to venture out to get her
soup. 'I'll deal with that when the time comes,' she thought.
Turning the page on her magazine, she promptly fell asleep.

'A good nap is one of the few blessings of old age,' she
would say upon awaking. But for now, the sweet dreams
would soothe her aching soul.

'Hi Estelle!' grinned Loveworthy. Her smile always
warmed Estelle's heart. This day was different though. She
could not find a smile to return to that sweet girl.

Unfazed, Loveworthy took Estelle's hand. 'You know,
I've been thinking,' she started. 'What your kids did to you
was outrageous! I still can't believe they did that!'

'Don't worry, child,' soothed Estelle. It was all she could
do to not cry in front of Loveworthy.

'No, Estelle, I am worried!' insisted Loveworthy. 'You
can't hide it from me. I know you are hurting! I'm so sorry!'

'Now child, you didn't do a darn thing.'

'But, I couldn't stop it! I didn't even know they did it until last week when I went to visit you and you were gone!' Loveworthy paused.

'I thought you had died, Estelle!' tears welling in her eyes. 'I thought you left me.'

'Never, child!' promised Estelle. 'I will never leave you! Now wipe that thought clean outa your silly-girl mind! Besides, that old house was getting to be too much trouble for these old bones. I could barely keep it clean without my hip going out.'

'It's better this way, reflected Estelle.' Looking around the barren, cold nursing home room, she forced a smile. 'See, I don't have nothin to clean here!'

'No, Estelle,' insisted Loveworthy. 'I refuse to believe that! You're just saying all that to make me feel better.' And before Estelle could respond, she continued, 'Estelle, I did something.'

'What?' asked Estelle, suspicious and not a little intrigued. 'What do you mean, you did something?'

'I found your daughter...' Loveworthy started.

'You did what?!' Estelle gasped. 'What do you mean...'

'I found Mabel'. Loveworthy's eyes twinkled, alerting Estelle to the possibility of another of Loveworthy's escapades. 'I got her to give me these,' she said, handing Estelle her house keys. 'You're going home!' exclaimed Loveworthy!

Just then, there was a knocking at the door.

'What is that knocking?' wondered Estelle. 'Be quiet! Loveworthy is breaking me out of the nursing home!'

Knock, knock, knock. 'Estelle, are you awake?' Hazel asked from behind the bedroom door.

Groggy, wiping spittle from her chin, Estelle sat up in her rocker and saw her magazine on the floor.

'Loveworthy,' she thought, longing to retreat to her dream.

Knock, knock, knock. 'Estelle,' called Hazel. 'Sorry to bother you, but it's breakfast time. Will you be joining us?'

'Go away!' shouted Estelle, to which Hazel responded by adding her name to the breakfast list.

'For the last time, I don't know why y'all is always pestering me!' grumbled Estelle, emerging at last from her bedroom.

'Can't even come out of my room to get cereal without, "Estelle, are you okay? Estelle, how are you? Estelle, this, Estelle that!" she snorted, winding up her legs to shuffle to the kitchen. 'Can't get a moment's peace around here!'

The women, gathered around the kitchen table for morning coffee, watched Estelle's entrance in silence. Rita grinned to herself, for she knew this was the opening to yet another Loveworthy story, as soon as Estelle could get out of her own way.

Thomasina walked to the cupboard for Estelle's favorite mug and met Estelle at the stove. 'Would you like some hot water, Estelle?' she asked. 'Hmph...yes, of course I want hot water! How else would the tea leaves steep?!' came the retort.

Thomasina smiled and set the water to cooking as Estelle found her private stash of tea, black tea, not that new age tea with all that stuff in it that shoulda stayed in the ground where it came from.

Finally, tea in hand, Estelle eyed the women and, as was her custom, decided to sit down with them. Her chair was open and waiting, her newspaper folded on her placemat. As she tottered to the table, the women resumed their morning chat. This day, the focus was on Hazel's granddaughter, who despite years of education and experience, couldn't find work.

Puzzled, Thomasina asked, 'Hazel, they say the economy is better than ever now. Unemployment is down. People are spending more. The housing market is stronger. There must be work out there for Jen.'

'I know. I don't get it either,' worried Hazel. 'I don't keep up on the news like you, Thomasina. All I know is that Jen is really smart. She got top grades in school. She is applying for jobs all the time. But, nothing comes through?!'

'Well,' started Rita, 'has she tried different kinds of work, or working for companies that she normally wouldn't consider? What I'm getting at is, maybe she needs to be creative about this. If the companies she used to work for don't need her skills, maybe others will. Or, maybe, she just has to repackage herself,' brainstormed Rita.

'She has been doing that, Rita. All last year, she was coming up with different strategies,' explained Hazel. 'That is not so much what worries me.'

'What is it then?' asked Thomasina, bringing muffins to table.

'It's that she's getting so depressed. She's losing her confidence. She told me the other day that she feels like an outsider, an outcast. She's embarrassed to be around her colleagues. She's avoiding getting together with friends because she is afraid they will ask her what she does and then she will have to tell them. She said she feels like a failure.' Hazel's voice trailed off, tears welling in her eyes.

Taking it all in, Estelle finally commented, 'Well, life don't always turn out the way it was supposta.'

'What do you mean, Estelle?' asked Thomasina, the only one brave enough to approach Estelle early in the morning.

Shooting a fiery look at Thomasina, Estelle held back her desire to leave and took a drink of her tea. 'I mean,' she stated with measured patience, 'Life is fulla disappointments. It's bitter sweet. I woulda told Jen, "Just deal with it and get on".' She paused. 'But Loveworthy...well, she thought differently.'

Grinning, Rita sat back with her coffee, awaiting the story.

KENTUCKY FRIED

'Loveworthy was always having get togethers,' smiled Estelle. 'I loved em cuz I didn't have to cook! And there was always such a bustle about, kids running this way and that, dressed as super heroes and Peter Pan. That Peter Pan outfit...' she trailed off, snickering.

Rita, seeing the imminent detour in Estelle's story, asked, 'So Loveworthy invited you to dinner?'

'Oh right, yes', startled Estelle. 'Well, you know Loveworthy was not what I call a cook. I mean, the kids was well fed and all. And, she tried really hard in the kitchen, but well, it's better soma us just don't set foot in there. But, like I said, I didn't have to cook, so I went.'

'This day, Loveworthy got in her head to cook a chicken, whole,' Estelle recalled. 'My ma taught me how to do that when I was just a girl, but I think Loveworthy's ma never got round to teaching her.'

'Oh oh, I know where this is going!' laughed Rita.

'So, Loveworthy announced that she was doin a experiment,' Estelle continued. 'She was gonna roast this chicken whole, complete with stuffin. She made the stuffin and went about cleaning the chicken. They is really slippery, ya know,' she said, to which the women nodded in agreement.

'Anyway, she couldn't get hold of that chicken and kept dropping it in the sink. I was tryin to tell her, but now her hands was all greasy and this time the chicken bounced in the sink! That was too much. I started laughing so hard, tears was rolling down my face. And Loveworthy, she was laughing too, grabbin that chicken everywhichway and dropping it!' laughed Estelle.

'I'm amazed she didn't rip it from limb to limb!' chortled Rita. 'Or strangle it!' Claire added, choking on her laughter.

'Well, she couldn't strangle it, cuz it didn't have no head,' Estelle corrected.

'That was a good thing!' laughed Rita. 'Imagine what she would have done with a head!' The women were on a roll now, savoring the levity of the moment, lusting after the freedom to simply laugh.

'You is right bout that, Rita,' Estelle granted. 'Loveworthy woulda had quite a time with a head.' 'So, then what happened?' encouraged Thomasina.

'Well, eventually the kids came in to see the bouncing chicken and the crazy ladies laughing. They danced around for a bit and then ran off. Last I heard, the girl was telling the little boy they oughta name their pet chicken.'

'Pet chicken??' asked Hazel. 'Why would they call it a pet chicken? It was dinner?!'

'Mind you, they was used to Kentucky Fried for dinner,' Estelle explained. 'They never seen a whole, real chicken. So, they thought to name their new pet.'

'Anyways, me and Loveworthy finally got aholda ourselves. And Loveworthy finally got aholda that bird. It was right clean by then. So she stuck it in the pot and stuffed it fulla that stuffing. She didn't know nothing bout tying the legs and I didn't want to boss her, so she stuck the whole thing in the oven, wings and legs poking out everywhichway.'

'We set the timer and went to find the kids. A little later, the timer went off so Loveworthy went to check the chicken. She was gone a long time. We was playing Monopoly. I hate that game?! And, it was Loveworthy's turn. So, the kids called her. They was getting crazy cuz she wasn't answering, so I went to get her.'

'I found Loveworthy in the kitchen, standing in front of the oven, staring.'

"It's alive," she whispered.

"What?!" I asked. "What's alive?"

"The chicken," she whispered, staring into the oven.

"Whachu sayin, girl?" I laughed. "That bird is dead as a doorknob! If it weren't dead when you got it, it was by the time you wuz done washing it!"

"No, Estelle! It's not dead?! Look!" So, I leaned over and looked. There it was, plain as day. "See," pointed Loveworthy. "Look, it's breathing."

'Sure enough, the chest was rising and falling, just like it was breathin?!'

'No way!' gasped Rita.

'Yes, it was breathin!' countered Estelle.

'But that always happens,' explained Thomasina. 'The liquid was boiling and causing the skin to rise and fall.' 'Yes,' agreed Hazel. 'I've seen that.' 'Me too,' agreed Claire. 'But it really does make the chicken look like it's breathing.'

'Now, that's a picture!' laughed Rita. 'A headless chicken, half cooked, in the oven, breathing!'

'Well, Loveworthy was just starring at it, not movin' said Estelle. 'And, as I watched, I saw the breathin was regular, steady, just like normal.' She sat silently, as if watching the chicken breathe. Then, 'pretty soon, the kids come runin in. They was tired of calling their ma and was arguing over who would take her turn.'

'They saw us standin there, so gathered all around us and looked into the oven. The biggest boy saw it first, "Ma, it's breathing." "See, I told you she is alive," said the little guy. "She is Chicky. And, she is alive." The girl just stood there, staring like her mother. "Ma!" cried the little boy, "We have to get Chicky out of the oven! She's getting too hot!"

'At this, Loveworthy broke out of her trance,' recalled Estelle. 'Without closing the oven door, she gathered her kids and asked about the Monopoly game. "No, we can't play now!" shouted the little guy. "We have to save Chicky first!" cried the girl. "Yeah, mom. That is pretty weird," agreed the oldest.

'So, Loveworthy took the chicken out of the oven as the kids watched. Then, relieved that Chicky was safe, they led us down to finish the Monopoly game.'

'Monopoly never ends!' claimed Rita. 'I've been in games that lasted days!' 'Me too,' agreed Claire and Hazel in chorus.

'After the kids got goin in the game again, Loveworthy snuck into the kitchen and put the chicken back in the oven. Later, when I was bout to explode from that damn game, Loveworthy called us all into dinner, thank god!' smiled Estelle.

'What Loveworthy couldn't do in the kitchen, she made up for in her table setting. She used her momma's dishes and silver and a pretty lace tablecloth she got from Goodwill. It was a right pretty table. There was sweet potatoes and stuffin and greens and milk for everyone. We all sat down. The kids was hungry.'

'Then, Loveworthy went to the kitchen. She came back with a carving knife and that chicken on a nice dinner plate. The kids was chattering bout who won the game when they all saw the bird. The older kids stopped talking. Then, the little guy recognized it and said, "Chicky?" The older kids looked from Chicky to Loveworthy. The little guy asked, "Mommy, why is Chicky on a plate?!"

'Loveworthy didn't respond. We all just sat there in silence. "Why isn't Chicky moving?" asked the little guy. Chicky just laid there, all dressed up and not breathin. Loveworthy weren't doin nothin and I was hungry, so I grabbed the carving knife and pulled Chicky to me.'

'Just as I was bout to carve up dinner, the little guy screamed, "Don't kill Chicky! Mommy, don't let 'stelle kill Chicky!" The girl said, "I'm not eating Chicky! How can I eat our pet?" And the oldest boy said, "I'm not really hungry, mom." The little boy was crying now, "Chicky, don't kill Chicky," he kept sayin. Estelle paused, lost in the memory.

'Well?' prompted Rita. 'What happened? Did you cut up that old bird?'

'No,' said Estelle. 'I didn't cut it up.'

'What about dinner?' asked Hazel. 'Didn't you all eat dinner?' 'Yes,' Estelle said, 'we ate the taters and greens. But we couldn't eat the stuffin that was in the bird cuz the biggest boy said we'd be gutting it if we did and that set the little boy to cryin again.'

'But, what about the bird?' insisted Rita. 'You didn't eat the bird?'

'No,' said Estelle. 'We never ate that bird. It just sat there in the middle of the table while we ate.'

'And then what? What became of the bird?' asked Hazel.

'We had a funeral,' stated Estelle. 'Chicky is buried in the backyard, stuffin and all, next to the bird and fish and cat and whatever else is buried back there.'

The women laughed, their faces lined with puzzlement. 'That's a great story, Estelle,' laughed Claire. 'Yes,' agreed Thomasina. 'And, the moral?' asked Rita.

'Well, it's what I said in the beginning,' reminded Estelle, 'Things don't always turn out the way they was supposta.' Looking at the confused women, Estelle continued, 'Me, I woulda told those kids that Chicky was dinner and cut up that chicken. But not Loveworthy.'

'Yes,' said Claire. 'I think Loveworthy saw something more in that bird, something more important than dinner.' 'What do you mean?' puzzled Hazel.

'She recognized that her kids were facing death for the first time,' stated Claire. 'Whoa!' started Rita, 'That's intense! It was dinner, for God's sake!'

'But, I think Claire's on to something,' said Thomasina. 'If all you ever ate was Kentucky Fried, would you know you were eating chicken?' 'Good point,' Rita agreed, 'and...'

'And,' continued Claire, 'correct me if I'm wrong here, Estelle, but I think Loveworthy decided that guiding her kids through their introduction to death was more important than eating that chicken.'

'So,' pondered Hazel, 'the original plan was to eat chicken for dinner.' 'Right,' said Claire.

'But,' chimed in Rita 'it turned into a lesson in life.' 'Right again,' smiled Claire.

'So,' offered Hazel, 'Loveworthy believed this lesson was more important than the money she spent on the chicken.'

'Yes, I think that's it,' affirmed Claire. 'And, she was able to step back from her original intention to allow a different course of events to flow,' added Thomasina.

'I think I get it,' reflected Thomasina. 'If she had perseverated on her idea that the chicken was dinner, she would have missed that unexpected and auspicious opportunity.'

In the following silence, Hazel ventured, 'So, do you think my granddaughter might be missing an opportunity...' she started. 'or something really important,' interrupted Rita. 'if she doesn't expand her thinking about how she can make a living,' Hazel finished.

'Perhaps,' agreed Thomasina. 'Or....' pondered Claire, 'if she gets too focused on feeling like a failure, she might forget that she really is a wonderful and talented young woman. And then, she won't reach for the possible because she won't believe in herself.'

'You're right,' reflected Hazel. 'Jen is a smart woman and very talented. She has so much to offer. She can't give up on herself, not now. But, maybe she needs to open herself up to see different opportunities and possibilities than she had originally expected.'

Claire turned to Estelle. 'What do you think? Are we understanding what you meant?'

'That's all too deep for me,' bristled Estelle. 'I just know that things don't always turn out the way they was supposta.'

With that, Estelle pushed herself up from the table and tottered off grumbling, 'It's always something! Estelle, this, Estelle that!' And, when her back was safely turned to the women, she smiled.

BEING GAY

I am deeply saddened to hear of the vicious attacks
against gay people around the world.
Though I have experienced this form of oppression,
oppression of any kind is a malicious assault on life.

I grieve for those who fear for their lives and families.
I pray for their safety and send them my love.

And, I grieve for those perpetuating this
horrible violence against humanity,
for they must live inside darkened hearts,
and fear that the hate they level against others
might be turned against themselves.

After all, hate is an equal opportunity scourge.
It will happily direct is enmity to anyone,
anywhere, for any reason.

We just need request its presence
and it springs forth, edgy and keen
for the promise of destruction and death.

I call now to all the gods and deities and spirits
that watch over the soul of humanity.

Please envelop us all - oppressors and oppressed alike –
in a blanket of love and compassion.

Show us the sacredness of those facing us.
Release us from the grip of hate and fear.
Teach us that difference and diversity
are essential to life.

Show us
how to celebrate difference,
how to see ourselves in another,
how to teach our children to love.

For, it is love that is our saving grace.
It is love that binds us all.
It is love, only love.

3 WARRIORS BORN OF DESTROYERS

A NEW SPIRIT GUIDE

There is a spirit whom I met just recently.
  She is ominous, portentous, outlandish,
  menacing and strange, so very strange.

She requires that I announce her presence,
  to share her audacious self with the world,
  to give voice to her warning and reproach.

But, her dark peculiarity challenges me
  so I have cowered, preferring instead
  a spirit less forbidding, more ordinary.

She presupposes my trepidation, yet
  has little patience for my reticence.
  So, I will try to share her with you.

BUT, BEFORE I BEGIN THIS STORY

Cailleach came to me during my
  two-year descent into poverty.

Her visits were unsolicited and startling.
  Her message was awful and distressing.

And try as I might, I couldn't escape her.
  She demanded that I give her voice.

She shares a devastating story of poverty,
  but promises abundance, if we can

  climb from our poverty of spirit.

THE CRONE

She has been coming to me in visions.
  She is a spirit guide, but not just for me.
  She has come for us all.

On the day we were to meet, I was taken to a dark place.
  Standing in the dark, I saw a rip in the fabric of reality.
  I was invited to tear the fabric, to step into the beyond.

So, I took hold of that vaporous rift and tore it asunder.
  Stepping inside, I found myself enveloped again in dark.
  I was in a dense forest, but not one of matter and flesh.

I stood alone, yet sensed beings all about me, watching.
  Then I saw, everywhere, flickering lights of many colors.
  And, I saw the lights were faeries, beautiful and dancing.

Though I have traveled far in spirit world, I have not
  allowed for interaction with this aspect of the mystic.
  I judged it harshly as childish, spurious and imaginary.

Yet there I was, watching faeries dance and light the dark,
  creating a delicate fabric of glistening beauty as they flew.
  Feeling overcome and incredulous, I ran from that world.

Silence fell.

The other day, I joined with a circle of friends to journey.
  I anticipated asking my spirit guides about my new book.
  Yet, I sensed the presence of a new spirit guide, waiting.

So, I journeyed to meet this spirit guide who awaited me.
  I was taken back to the portal between the two realities.
  Once inside, I saw radiant colors illuminating the dark.

And, I sensed a presence.
  Turning, I saw her floating just above the ground.
  And what I saw next shocked and flummoxed me.

She was wearing a Steampunk Ball Gown, a hoop dress.
  All white, layers of ruffles folded one upon the other,
  ascending the vast expanse from her feet to her waist.
  A lace and satin bodice sat atop this peculiar costume.

Looking to the figure it framed, I saw a very old woman.
  Her face was gaunt and, well, ugly. Her nose protruded
  over stern lips, hid eyes sunken deeply in the gaunt skull.

Her hair, scant and disheveled, was tucked awkwardly in
  a regal Juliette Cap that sat askance on her balding head.
  Her hands bore long, bony fingers and she was barefoot!

Stunned, I gaped at this bizarre figure as she glared at me.
  I emerged from the journey astonished and incredulous.
  This message came to me.

She is the Crone, extravagant, effusive, lavish, audacious,
  regal, gaudy, daring, bold, powerful, playful, adventurous.
  This is a theater in which to create. 'Do not oppose me!'

She is here. She has announced her garish self to the world.
  I am almost afraid to ask the purpose of our rendezvous.
  She bears tidings. How can one so audacious not speak?

ÉLAN VITAL: YOUR LIFE IN A BREATH

I was sent back to the darkness.
  I saw the slips of color all round me
  and the spirit, magnificent, noble, extravagant.

She transformed into a woman my age.
  Her demeanor was compassionate, loving, kind.
  She took my hand and we walked in the darkness.

Freed from the prison of my disbelief,
  the slips of color transformed into faeries.
  They danced all about us, enfolding us in color.

Then, the darkness rolled back from the land,
  revealing lush forest, alive and sparking with energy.
  Each flower, each blade of grass was a faery transformed.

The Crone merged with me, touched my soul.
  I felt a profound love, a knowing, a deep peace.
  And, the energy that is me swelled and fomented.

Then, the world changed.

The material dissolved, becoming diaphanous.
  Every thing transformed into luminescent energy.
  Vibration and light defined flowers, rocks and streams.

Energy surged through the trees
  and exploded out the thousands of leaves.
  Energetic cords reached from roots into the earth.

The gossamer cords grew below the earth,
   flowing, exploring, connecting, dancing, playing
   in a pulsating, vibrant web of intentionality, of creation.

Then, I saw the energy that was my body.
   And, I saw the energetic cords that held my form
   to this earth even as I raised my feet from the ground.

Lifting my gaze, I saw the energetic web
   connecting all things, flowing between forms,
   holding shape as if in response to a game challenge.

Élan Vital,
   the vital force, the impulse of life.
   Élan Vital, the creator and the creation.

My life, your life,
   the form we call 'me',
   what we share and receive,
   our lives, the steps on our paths,
   all ONE with the impulse of life, Élan Vital.

Élan Vital,
   the in breath, the out breath,
   the chi, the ALL, your life in a breath.

CAILLEACH: DAUGHTER OF THE WINTER SUN

I told my friend about the strange new spirit guide.
   Stunned, she exclaimed, 'You are describing Cailleach!'
   She showed me a description and portrayal of this spirit.

Astonished at the striking resemblance to my visions,
   I sought to learn if Cailleach was indeed this new spirit.
   Everything I read confirmed her as the spirit in my visions.

These things I learned about this ancient goddess, Cailleach.

She is known as the Daughter of the Winter Sun, the Crone,
   the Dark Mother, the gigantic Hag, the Harvest Goddess,
   the Goddess of Death, the Old Woman of Knowledge.

Mother to gods and goddesses, grandmother to humanity.
   Guardian of the equilibrium between humanity and nature.
   Goddess of the portal linking realms of humanity and spirit.

Cailleach is extremely powerful and demands respect.
   If you cross her, she will mete out consequences.
   She can invoke love or terror, hope or dread.

Goddess of Transformation,
  she culls the dead and brings new life.
  She ushers in winter and delivers the spring.

CAILLEACH: SHE WILL NOT BE DENIED

This is the spirit of my visions, this Cailleach.

The awe and wonderment of meeting her
  is surpassed only by my instinct to be wary.

Each time she presents herself, I retreat,
  needing time for repair, to catch my breath.

Her presence, her power, her intent, all
  are perplexing, unnerving and disconcerting.

Yet even when I steer clear of her, she sows phantasmagorias
  in my mind and scatters words from my fingers to the page.

Next I sat with my circle, I chose to drum rather than journey.
  Daunted at meeting Cailleach yet again, I cowered from her.

Later, relieved at having circumvented another encounter,
  I sat listening to my friend's reflections on their journeys.

No sooner than quiet fell, Cailleach collided with my world,
  and pen met paper to pronounce the messages she brings.

CAILLEACH'S WRATH

Her anger coalesced into form.
  Mountains shook, oceans swelled.
  Winds whipped into deadly cyclones.

'I awake from my slumber to discover
  you have desecrated this sacred ground!!'
  I hear naught but her terrible, deafening scream.

Her eyes, torrents of abhorrence and ferociousness,
  level on me, insignificant, inferior, a minor blip in life.
  As I slouch in fear, she draws near, eyes piercing my soul.

'Human kind is a pernicious pestilence polluting this ground!
  In a single epoch, humanity slaughters the mother of its soul!
  Can you not see you have laid waste to life itself?' she shouts.

'The creatures depart forever. Their spirits hasten to my side.
  Can you identify all you have slaughtered in your indolence?
  Can you not see the vital roles they play in the web of life?!'

Gathering courage, I plead in defense of my sullied species.
  'Yes, we are responsible for the ruin. But, we are young.
  We have lost our way. Please, take pity on us, please!'

'Only your extermination will release this earth from
  the plague that is humankind!' Cailleach exclaims.
  'It is a fool's errand that you ask me to follow!'

'Please!' I cry, shamed by our brazen disregard
  for the precious gift of life, terrified by the
  blight we have set lose upon this earth.

'I bring winter to the world,' she asserts.
  'I will arrest the process of life, itself,
  to purge the curse that is humanity.'

THE ACCOUNTING

Flying above the earth,
  terrible mien, sharp eyes,
  sledgehammer at the ready.

Searching for the pestilence,
  intent on eradicating the blight,
  determined to rescue the creatures.

Considering drawing close the veil of life,
  lowering the shroud over our unseeing eyes,
  disconnecting us, forever, from Élan Vital, life.

Her countenance is hostile, unforgiving, severe.

She appeals to the stones by name. They move.
  At her bid, mountains heave and oceans part,
  exposing our disgrace, revealing our crimes.

She sets loose winter's ire upon humanity.
  After it cleanses the human scourge,
  the winter of our souls will begin.

And, it will have no end.

THE BLACK BOX

What to do with her fury?
  I speak it,
  but it frightens me.

My soul grows cold.
  I hide,
  but I find no safety.

Nor can you.
  No one,
  none is safe now.

All your wealth,
  a black box,
  empty, worthless.

Awaken, awaken!
  Life is wealth.
  Invest in life, now.

The black box
  of greed.
  Open it, let it go.

Flood the black box
  with light.
  Shine it on the world.

Lay your hand
  upon life.
  Give. Gift. Now.

Feel the Source
  within you.
  Act upon it. Now.

Now, Now,
  Now,
  Now, Now, Now.

SHE SPEAKS

These words from Cailleach.

'Brilliance cast from a distant love
  showers through me,
  spreading from this universe to the next.'

'It sits in the base of your spines.
  You know it as Kundalini.
  It animates all life.
  It is the chi, the ALL.'

'It infuses the earth, lives deep within its core,
  awaits your humble acknowledgement of
  the plague you set lose upon this world.'

'The answer is among you, in you.
  YOU are the answer.'

Cailleach transforms again into the
  mother of spring, hope and compassion.
  Her enmity melts into a timeless love for all life.

Wrapped in our shroud of arrogance and ignorance,
  we stand amid the destruction we have wreaked on earth.
  The Old Woman of Knowledge extends her love, even to us.

Dance with her, feel her spirit alive in you.
  Remember, we have always been part of the ALL.
  The walkers, slitherers, flyers, swimmers, the rooted, us…

We, the lost children, are welcomed back.
  The table of life is set, our transgressions forgiven.
  All life, animate and inanimate, awaits our humble petition.

Dare to look beyond the dirt that holds together this body,
  to the soul, the spirit, the chi that animates all life.
  Feel the hope, the love of which we are made.

There.
  Feel it.
  It vibrates.
  It is luminescent.
  It is God, Allah, the ALL, the ONE.

Step back from the brink of arrogance.
  Feel the ocean. Hear the wind.
  Remember, remember.

Her terrible countenance softens.
  She reaches her hand to us in love.
  She waits for us to take just one step.

She will respond to even the smallest step.
  She will assist us to bridge the horrible schism
  we fashioned between ourselves and all other life.

But she will not dwell long in this hiatus.
  She holds winter in her other hand, and
  she will lay waste to all if we cannot find
  the humility and the resolve to step forth.

We are the only ones who can bring an end
  to the terrible desolation and destruction.
  Not our children, nor their children.

No, it must be us.

BECOME, NOW

Look out,
  beyond yourself,
  into the universe.

Eyes closed,
  vision clear, strong.
  All will be revealed.

For you,
  and for them.
  Yes, them too.

Hearts open,
  love pours in,
  envelopes you.

Love is
  the answer
  to all questions.

You are
  made from love
  You ARE love.

All fear,
  enemy of love,
  desecrator of life.

KRISTEN MÄGIS

Fear is
  anger, envy,
  resentment,
  bitterness,
  antipathy,
  prejudice,
  intolerance,
  bigotry.

Fear breeds
  discrimination,
  power over,
  injustice,
  inequality,
  injury,
  hunger,
  death...

You are
  made from love.
  You ARE love.

Allow love
  to expose
  all your fears.

Ask love
  to quiet
  your fearful heart.

Bequeath love
  on those
  you know not.

Stand up
  to the dark
  with your light.

Take back
  our humanity
  Take our place.

In life,
  we are born
  protectors, gifters.

For life,
  be
  the gift of love.

Winter settles
  upon the earth.
  Too late to stop.

Cailleach
  has sent
  the frost, cold.

Take heed.
  It is not
  over, only cold.

Life begs
  our complete
  courage, heart.

Become
  who you were
  meant to be, love.

Together,
  let us all
  save this earth.

Our gift
  is our essence,
  love come alive.

STEP OUT OF SLUMBER INTO YOUR BIRTHRIGHT

Glaciers heave,
  waters freeze,
  cities fall dark.

Cailleach will
  leave none untouched
  by her cold, hard fury.

Are you frightened?
  If you are, you have woken up!
  The veil has been lifted, and
  you have been gifted with sight.

Just in time
  to see the world fall
  into death's dark abyss.
  The pause threatened by
  Cailleach is upon us, now.

Don't close your eyes!
  Don't run back to the fantasy
  of self-imposed ignorance or denial!

You will not find safety there!
  It is just a delusion that allows
  murder and darkness to descend.

No! Force your eyes open!
  Only with clear sight can you
  step into the sacred role reserved
  for humanity in this crisis of our making.

Stay awake! Stay present!
  The shock, the dismay, the terror
  at seeing the consequence of our crimes
  is natural. Its gift is to inspire our urgency.

Staying awake will enable you to act!
  It will allow you to see others,
  equally awake and seeking.

It will break down boundaries
  and allow the vital gift of love
  to reinvigorate broken bonds.

It will create clarity of perception
  so that we can use our distinctive
  gifts of innovation and creation
  to find our way through the winter.

The winter calls forth warriors,
  not mindless soldiers, but deeply
  contemplative warriors, honor-bound
  by the simple and universal call to love.

Recall the great warriors from your lineage;
  clarity of vision, giant hearts, soulful eyes,
  called to a purpose greater than self-interest,
  inclusive of all, great and small, life, love.

That is the warrior in you!
  All are called to awaken, now,
  to step into the armor of love.

That is your calling!
  This is your birthright!
  Warriors, all.

We will be gifted
  courage, sight, capabilities
  as we call them forth for good.

There is no greater calling
  than to become what we
  were born to be, a gift to life,
  warriors of love, creators all.

The Great Slumber is over.

We awaken.
  We accept our birthright.
  We carry the mantle of love.
  We don our armor.
  We birth the answers.
  We gift ourselves
  to life.

4 STRENGTH BORN OF WEAKNESS

WATCH, LISTEN, LEARN

Watch, listen with your heart.
  I load the new wash machine
  and watch to see how it works.

It launches by sensing the load.
  It tests the load gingerly at first,
  slight movements of the washer.

The washer sways back and forth,
  gauging the weight, the balance,
  the proportion of this new load.

Then it takes a test spin,
  centrifugal force holding
  clothes against the drum.

Finally, arriving at an understanding
  of its load, the washer commences
  the cycle to launder my garments.

And then I realize,
  I am starting a new chapter in life.
  I must pause to sense the load.
  I need to witness Spirit move.

STRENGTH IN WEAKNESS

I was journeying to my ancestors,
   seeking the shaman of my lineage,
   requesting help from my spirit guides.

'Your heart is weak,' they declared.
   'What?' I asked, startled.

'Your heart is weak,' they repeated.
   'Wait, what?!'

Silence

Three weeks later, the doctor stated,
   'You must see a cardiologist.
   Your heart is weak.'

'What?!'

In journey circle,
   I spoke the words
   'My heart is weak?!'

In tears, I journeyed
   to this shocking truth,
   unsure even what to ask.

I found in that sacred space
   a wild boar, ferocious visage,
   menacing bearing, glaring at me.

No weaponry, no recourse, no escape.
   I faced the wild boar, gazed into my peril.
   Suddenly, a profound peace filled my heart,
   infused my spirit, enveloped my terrified being.

As I stood exposed to the ravages of this monster,
   Spirit revealed two hearts beating within my frame,
   a physical heart, the one that is damaged and failing,
   and a spiritual heart, the one that dwells beyond time.

Then, Spirit gathered my broken heart into its arms
   and, embracing it compassionately, revealed that
   the strength of my spiritual heart would heal it.

Strength in weakness.

ONLY TO WITNESS AND FEEL

In the brutal moment that lasted an eternity,
  I learned what it is like to die, and, to die alone.

Collapsed on the floor, unable to move.
  Observing my inert body from the outside.

The tether holding my soul to my body stretching.
  The soul detaching, the body heaving to pull it back.

Unable to move, only to witness and feel.

SETTLING INTO A NEW REALITY

A week later and it is staring to make sense.
  The crushing of my heart during hot flashes,
  the swollen ankles, the never-ending exhaustion,
  the chest pains when I walk, climb stairs, lay down.

Now the memories are surfacing.
  My mother fighting for life after heart surgery.
  My father dying following the heart procedure.
  My mother-in-law dying after the heart surgery.

Another hot flash.
  Another constriction of the heart.
  The pain spreads throughout my chest.
  Oh my god! This is real! This is really real!

There are stages in the grieving process,
  denial, anger, bargaining, depression, acceptance.
  Grieving is a normal process through which we pass
  when life transforms the unimaginable into the absolute.

I recognize them, have walked through them many times.
  I expect to pass through them again with this new reality.
  But, there is something fundamentally different this time.

I am aware of, can feel more regularly, the hand of Spirit,
  a deep sense of peace, a strength of heart, an acceptance
  of the next stage in this journey of my soul on this plane.

Facing death, my mother could choose to live or die.
  Choosing life, she wasted not a moment of her days.
  Like my mother, I choose to live into every moment.

I choose to be as fully present as I can, to imagine the
  impossible, to seek opportunities to live my purpose,
  to accept wisdom, to love and live with all that I am.

ALLOW ME TO HEAL THE SORROW

Spirit calls to me,
  'Through pain and sorrow, I offer healing.
  I heal the pain. Yet, you hold the sorrow.'

'A new morning dawns,' says Spirit.
  'The threat of homelessness is gone.
  Food is on the table. Income is secured.'

'I urge you to rejoice in the new space.
  I invite you to celebrate this moment.
  I ask you to give form to your dreams.'

'Yet, you resist.'

'It is the memories that hold you back.
  Feelings of loss, rejection, separation.
  And the fear these gifts are transient.'

'So, you grasp your sorrow, cleave to it.
  You believe that releasing it is dangerous,
  will bring back the pain, the chaos, the fear.'

'Look,' admonishes Spirit.

'Sit quietly, feel Me, know that I AM here.
  I bring you wisdom, and the ability to integrate
  knowledge and experience with divine inspiration.'

'Look to Me, see the vastness of the All,
  the connection of every being and thing.
  There is no them, no us, no separation.'

'Look deeply into and beyond your experience.
  Seek the wisdom I offer, that you can find only
  by experiencing the material, living fully, openly.'

'In the depths of your soul, you will find Me.
  I AM always here, with you, forever more.
  Seek Me and you shall find Me - always.'

'Open your heart to Me, completely.
  Allow Me to heal your sorrow
  so you can live fully into
  each blessed moment.'

SAFETY FROM HARM

The overwhelming feeling of needing to cry.
 From where? For what? I do not know.
 But the sorrow is deep, so very deep.

Spirit chides,
 'You cling to your sorrow like a child,
 grasping the hem of her mother's dress.
 So frightened are you to let go, to feel Me.'

I explain,
 'I yearn for security, feel desperately a need
 for safety from harm. If I release my grip,
 I will step into harm's way. I will be hurt!'

'The security you grasp for is an illusion.
 You misconstrue familiarity with security.
 You are holding onto old pain, sorrow, fear.'

Seeking wisdom, I listen to the words of Spirit,
 Negotiating, 'OK, if I let go my hold on fear,
 I will fall into the safety of your arms, right?'

I imagine letting loose my clutch on the old.
 I see myself, safe and secure in Spirit's arms.
 I feel ready, at last, to release my hold on fear.

'My child, it is not about moving from one notion
 of safety to another. That logic allows fear to
 preserve its rule over your heart and mind.'

'It is about letting go of the fear, totally.
 It is about stepping into your future
 without a script written by fear.'

'Only then can you experience the splendor
 of this Spirit walk, the magnificence of Creation,
 and the wisdom you have sought these many years.'

'Step into your future, the unknown, without the
 the incessant search for safety from harm.
 There is no harm, no need for security.'

'Step out of the illusion and into Me.'

EFFORTLESS, GRACEFUL

I was standing in a desert.
  Gauze covered my body
  and wafted in the breeze.

Sand dunes all around.
  Wind blowing against my face.
  'Turn to see where the wind blows.'

As I turned, Tortoise
  ascended beneath my feet,
  lifting me gently off the sand.

With majestic, measured stokes,
  she took to flight above the earth.
  Wind at my back, breeze on my face.

Then, she dove into the sand dune.
  Sand flowed across my feet and ankles.
  Arms outspread, head high, atop my friend.

She plunged more deeply into the earth.
  Dirt flowed past my shins, my knees, my waist.
  Her stride unbroken, steady, constant, inexhaustible.

She advised, 'If you resist, you will grow weary.'
  'Allow life to flow. Do not resist. Do not fight.'
  Long, steady, unhurried, mindful, effortless strokes.

Tortoise swam effortlessly in enormous circles,
  flying through the dirt as an eagle through the sky.
  The pressure of the earth against my body lessened.

'Swim,' she instructed.
  So, I let go just above her mighty shell.
  I mimicked her strokes, strong, slow, steady, mindful.
  I was swimming through the earth, gracefully, effortlessly.

When I grew tired, I rested on her shell.
  She continued to swim, now to the stars.
  It is all the same to her, earth, stars, ocean.

'Resistance is a state created by our minds.
  It is a primal game played by our minds with
  the most elementary of emotions, fear,' she said.

111

'Let go your resistance,' she counseled.
  'Rejoice in the flow of life about your feet.
  Revel in your ability to fly through all of life.

'And, never fear,
  for fear chokes your breath,
  shackles your feet, steals your vision.'

A CALL TO PEACE

A feeling so big, it expands beyond me.

It wants to explode out and beyond.
  It commands freedom from the
  limits and failings of my mind.

It wants to show the magnificence,
  to share the wonder, the awe.
  It wants to point to the All,

'Look beyond, into!' it shouts.

'Look and see
  the holy that is your self!'

'Feel the immense joy
  of knowing you are
  at one,
  always,
  with the All!'

'Breathe lightly.
  Experience profound peace.
  Let yourself fall into the ecstasy
  of pure, unconditional, eternal love.'

WHO YOU ARE IN THE PASSING

Spirit whispered yesterday, resounding
  through the din of my mind at work.

'You are here only briefly, then gone.
  Your triumphs will vanish with time.'

'Remember, at the close of your life,
  it is not your work that will matter.'

'Rather,
  it is who you were in the passing.'

It Was a Strange Little Journey

Walking this new path.
  Striving to savor the gifts.
  Struggling with my own resistance
  to release the old, to embrace the new.

When suddenly,
  everything changed.
  I lay on the kitchen floor,
  feeling my soul leave my body.

Several heart beats later,
  an ambulance chauffeured me
  to a hospital bed, nurses, doctors,
  tests, sleepless nights, IVs, medicine...

Upon my release, I was
  whisked to a heart surgeon,
  who set in motion the medical
  machine, tests, procedures, more tests...

Caught up in the whirlwind,
  I acquiesced, allowed the tests.
  But, something else was stirring,
  something beyond this physical plane.

It announced, 'I am done with this.'
  Its strength grew even as my body failed.
  It persevered as the fog lifted from my mind.
  It pressed forward and activated the Kundalini.

It suggested that I could heal myself.
  The corporeal experience is the stage
  on which it will reveal itself and its gifts.
  I simply need to listen, witness and allow.

Kundalini Healing

Something shifted.
  Like a groundswell, it quaked my being,
  woke me up, turned me bout, faced me forward.

It left me knowing I'm done with the incident
  that landed me in the medical machine.
  And, it left me with a realization
  that I can heal myself.

Yes.

Kundalini awoke two nights ago.
  It emerged in the evening,
  and then became quiet
  until I lay to rest.

My hand,
  resting on my abdomen,
  awoke it, once again.

It stirred and stretched
  into my abdomen, awaking
  the organs, innervating them,
  activating frenzied movement.

My body then flushed itself,
  cleansed itself of the toxins.
  I lay again to rest, reflecting.

Several hours later,
  the Kundalini stirred again,
  exploded through my viscera,
  wrapped my abdomen in energy.

Twice, in succession, it awakened,
  then shot up my chakras to my heart,
  surrounding it, impregnating my chest
  with swirling, healing, intentional energy.

I slept then, with powerful dreams,
  the remnants of which float through
  the recesses of my mind, occasionally
  surfacing, offering gifts and promise.

I feel well, over the medical incident.
  I feel filled with a powerful something.

I feel profound gratitude and an attitude,
  an impatience, an excitement, an arrogance,
  a restlessness, a humble realization that my ego
  has been stimulated and is trying to claim its space.

So into quiet I must fall, for Spirit is trying to teach me.
  Please help me to listen, to hear, to learn what You offer.

FROLIC!

How much of our lives do we
  NOT really pay attention
  to the magic in the air?

That's it, you know.
  It is magic.
  Or, so it seems.

Synchronicities abound.
  Like subatomic particles,
  appearing, dissolving, flying,
  colliding, combining, creating.

Everything we need to know.
  All that we need to grow.
  Anything we need.
  It is all there.

Sometimes,
  life grabs you,
  turns you bout face,
  demands that you look.

And in the quiet, it shows
  you the wonder, the elegance,
  the magnificence of this experiment.

So, when you hear the call, find quiet.
  Seek, behold the All in your self.
  And, frolic in the sacred dance.

Yes, frolic! It is a gift, just for you!
  Dance, sing, laugh, witness the beauty.
  Know that you are full, whole, well, healed.

Then, feel gratitude, give thanks, offer your self
  to the deep healing needed in this world.
  Be part of the synchronicity, the hope.

EVERYTHINGNESS

The black box.
  That is me.

Turning, floating.
  Solid, evanescent.

All round, nothing.
  Or is it everything?

Searching for the opening.
  Finding none, needing none.

Watching the atoms melt.
  Watching the box dissolve.

Into the nothingness,
  everythingness.

The black box, a facade.
  No, a journey, an experience.

Not the full reality.
  Not even me.

An invitation,
  to explore, adventure, learn, feel.

And just for a moment.
  Do not let it pass unaware.

ONLY I

You need not safety,
  for there is no such thing as harm.

Only IS

You need not fear,
  for there is nothing to fear.

Only I

TRANSCENDENCE

I so wanted everything to be okay.
  It was just a blip, a convergence of
  menopause stuff, a migraine, a virus...
  all of which disturbed an ailing heart.

But, it wasn't.

The heart valve is not well.
  And, its dysfunction is now
  affecting other organs, creating
  affliction where once there was vigor.

Many feelings to accept and honor.
  Then, I must initiate preparations,
  putting all in order for my family.

I will continue the healing process.
  I will live life fully, each moment.
  I will love fully and with abandon.
  I will give thanks for every breath.

DIVINE GRACE

It was just one week ago that I sat
  with the Cardiac Surgeon, stunned.
  'You must have heart surgery, soon.'

And, just in case my desire to deny
  this reality overtakes my judgment,
  my heart supplies regular reminders.

The new symptoms present even before
  I have adjusted to the current symptoms,
  or integrated the changes into my lifestyle.

The events of the last month have cast me
  in the role of constantly chasing to catch up
  with a reality that is unfolding with authority,
  determination, precision and unyielding intent.

I am trying to adjust, to prepare, to make plans.
  But the heart struggles, with each beat, to endure.
  Tears of fatigue, agony, frustration, confusion, grief.

Then, the loving, gentle voice in the chaos.
  'You are resisting. You are trying to control
  that which is beyond you. Let go, completely.'

All day, that voice captures my heart and soul.
  In conversation, gasping for breath, feeling dizzy...
  Through it all, the loving, quiet, yet persistent counsel.

'Release, surrender all of you, totally and without reserve.'
  Find quiet. Trust in the unfolding. Allow. Witness.
  For this is a sacred time, a time in which Spirit
  is fully present and intentionally engaged.'

I hear.
  I hear you.
  I am listening.

And the tears flowed,
  in reaction to the dawning that 'this really is real?!';
  in response to the compassion shown by so many;
  in surrendering the need to control, to understand.

I am thankful for the lessons presented for my ascension.
  Yet, I wonder what is so important that it necessitates
  this profound cleansing to transpire with such haste.

I am understanding healing at profound level.
  Healing the physical heart is just the beginning.
  Healing spans the ages, weaves through physical,
  emotional, intellectual, and reaches to the heavens.

It is Spirit,
  animating this flesh,
  surging through this life
  with a force and intention
  we can only start to envision,
  but never, really, comprehend.

It is the All, fully present,
  always engaged, forever love,
  incomprehensible, eternal, ALL.

I am in awe, in love, profoundly grateful,
  stunned by the magnificence, humbled by
  this journey on which I am but a passenger.

To this journey, I surrender my being.
  I ask for the courage, peace and wisdom
  to let myself fall, fully and without reserve,
  into Divine Grace.

MINIATURE ASSASSIN

I do have a fear.

In the shadow of the furor and fuss about the heart,
  grows a small but deadly plaque on the carotid artery.
  It resides at the base of the skull, inches from my brain.

I have not allowed myself to acknowledge the fear
  incited through my being by this miniature assassin.
  Even positive thinking can be used to hide from reality.

And, hiding is exactly what I have been doing of late.
  So, brutal honesty. I am horrified by the possibility of
  having a debilitating stroke, losing my ability to cogitate.

My mind is my greatest strength. From it flows my gift.
  This gift, my writing, requires a mind capable of discerning
  the perfect word to weave into an exquisite phrase, a thought.

Without my mind, I am a painter without a paintbrush.
  Without words to express that which cries for expression,
  I am as a songbird without a voice, a ballerina without legs.

I can imagine no greater assault to my being than to
  lose my mind, lose my gift, be forced to live robbed
  of the ability to think.

My mother almost died from a stroke during heart surgery.
  My father died from an aneurysm during a pre-heart surgery
  procedure. My grandmother and grandfather died from strokes.

I have always known this was likely to be my demise.
  I never imagined that it could come at 54-years-old.
  I live a healthy life style. I care for my body.

So, what to say after acknowledging the fear in my heart?
  I shall not chide myself nor shirk in shame at expressing fear.
  I shall stay with it, love it, and honor it. Then, I shall seek quiet.

And, I shall await the Divine Grace upon which I rely for all.

IT IS FINAL

Suddenly struck with a profound feeling of sadness.

Regardless of the new soul journeys awaiting me,
sadness suffuses my being with the passing of this life.
I feel immense sorrow in leaving this place, this existence.

The people, the undone business, the intentions,
my grandchildren, born and waiting to arrive,
my children, the future we might have had...

A stroke denying me the ability to communicate
feels also as a death, perhaps even worse.
The grief leaves a bilious feeling in me.

There is no coming back from death.
It is final.

I want to face this possibility,
to allow my responses to it,
to honor the feelings, fully.

DOES VICTORY REQUIRE AN 'OVER'?

Does victory require an 'over'?
Victory over...
Victory over death.

But, death is not an enemy.
It is, like all of this life, simply
a transition from this to the next.

Death is part of life.
It is as fundamental as
birth, breath, love, belief...

There is no need to vanquish death.
And, to celebrate 'victory over death' is
as senseless as rejoicing 'victory over birth'.

All is one, all is Divine, sacred.
Death, life, all...is transformation.
From then to now, from here to there.

The victory is not in conquering.
Victory is living intentionally
through the entirety of it.

YOU ARE YOUR FATHER'S DAUGHTER

This was the weekend of my father's birth and passing.
  Many emotions emerged, some enigmatic and painful to
  unpack, all intricately woven into my relationship with him.

It started Friday in mediation with a deep-seated sorrow.
  I sat with the sorrow, explored its depth and expanse.
  In the quiet, I was shown its birth and life source.

The sorrow is my deep disappointment in myself.
  As I face my mortality, I am acutely aware
  that I never measured up to my father.

My earliest memories include looking at my father
  and seeing a hero. I witnessed his impact on all who
  stood in his presence, his incredible contribution to life.

And I wanted nothing more than to be like him.
  I wanted to create something that touched people's
  hearts and souls, and left an indelible mark on their lives.

I wanted to have people love and seek me out,
  just as they did him. 14 years after his passing,
  they express their devotion to and love for him.

I wanted to grow wise and compassionate.
  I wanted my children to cherish my counsel.
  I wanted them to regard me as a wise mother.

My sorrow is born of my belief that to
  live a life of value means that
  I must be like my father.

Its source of nourishment has been the constant
  reminder that I am not like him, that I have always
  and continue to, fall short of the life he demonstrated.

In the abyss created by the possibility that few days remain,
  the long-standing fear that I do not measure-up quickened
  into trepidation that it could materialize and define my life.

Then, in the quiet of the candle light and my tears, I heard,
  'But you are not your father. His journey is not to be yours.'
  The words, scarcely audible above my heart keening, lingered.

Two days later, driving my grandson home,
  we listened to melodies from 'The Lion King'.
  It evoked a poem I wrote to honor my parents.

My father, like Simba's father, left a huge footprint in life.
  I recounted how I accidentally stepped into my father's
  footprint and found myself swallowed in its immensity.

Years later, I still can't find my way out of that huge footprint.
  And the quiet voice repeated, 'You are not your father.'
  You were never meant to journey on his path.'

'While you mourn that for which you were never destined,
  you miss the journey that is yours to walk in this life.
  You are your father's daughter. Your life matters.'

'You have sown seeds of love. There are those who love you.
  You have gifted to life and can as long as chi fills your heart.'

I am my father's daughter.
  I am not done contributing to life.
  I can love, and gift, and offer my heart.

So, I will.

JUST REGULAR

Spirit offers, 'Be, simply be.'

I laugh, 'But, I am just regular.'
  'That is just enough,' smiles Spirit.

'Regular is inadequate,' I challenge.
  Spirit cheers, 'Regular is magnificent!'

Pressing, I complain, 'I want more than regular.'
  Patiently, Spirit asks, 'What is it you want, then?'

'I want to shine, brightly,' I announce.
  Spirit applauds, 'Then shine for all to see!'

Shrinking into doubt, 'But, I'm just regular...'
  Holding my heart, 'And yet, your light shines.'

COURAGE, WRAPPED IN A YOUNG WOMAN

I did a training session on leadership the other day.
  It started with John Wayne riding off into the sunset
  after once again single-handedly conquering the bad guys.

This story has inflicted immeasurable damage
  on the self-image of countless people, robbing
  them from discovery of their inherent greatness.

Beleaguered by a diminished sense of self-efficacy,
  they cower from expressing their personal greatness,
  preferring to hide behind self-criticism and other-adulation.

In this demoralizing story, people are born to be common,
  some more so than others, young women for example.
  Life conspires to keep them from shining their light.

This plight leads me directly to the topic of courage.
  To step outside what is expected of you, to reach,
  to have the audacity to believe you can be more...

This requires courage, in the truest sense of the word.
  Because, you see, courage is not reaching for that which
  you know you can do, or have the wherewithal to achieve.

Courage is daring to step into the mystery, even when you
  feel ill-equipped to do so, without the guarantee of success,
  and especially when you have struggled in previous attempts.

True courage requires no small amount of faith and daring.
  It requires readiness to fail countless times before victory.
  It requires humility in the face of this daunting challenge.

There is a person about whom I think when I ponder courage.
  That person is my daughter, a beautiful young woman who
  has suffered multiple blows in the pursuit of her dreams.

Despite the challenges and her past experiences, she
  dares to step, once again, onto the path to her dream.
  She knows the journey isn't easy, but is committed to it.

She takes the risk, accepting the failures with the successes.
  She faces her fears and dares to walk with and despite them.
  This is courage personified, in the flesh, in real life, in action.

We don't know what lies ahead of us, or within ourselves.
  But, we are called to search for and discover our greatness.
  Then seek to live and give to life with the all of who we are.

DEFINING MOMENTS

I am struck lately with the presence of certain moments.
  These moments stand apart from all others in our lives.
  Their resolve to be recognized is absolute, unwavering.

These moments change lives, turn us inside out,
  leave us breathless or crushed or astonished or...
  They ask us to wake up, pay attention, closely.

They seem as harbingers of a new day dawning.
  They are an instrument of our souls beckoning
  us inward into stillness, into keen wakefulness.

Therein, we are endowed with gifts styled for that moment.
  We are offered the perfect measure of everything we need.
  And the chisel will be set to the stone, creating us de novo.

We are never finished being born.

And, those precious, perplexing, wondrous moments are
  the vessels, ingredients and the alchemy of our unfolding.
  These are the defining moments, the gifts offered to us all.

DIVINE SPARK

I am but a spark in the Divine mystery.
  I know not of the future nor the past.
  But, I shall shine brightly and boldly
  for as many days as this life shall last.

ANGER

I feel angry this morning.

Having procrastinated until the last moment,
  I now must ensure my last will and testament
  is complete so that I can show it to my children.

The child in me wants to jump up and down,
  tear into God about the insanity of this journey,
  question, challenge, denounce the reality-unfolding.

I do not want to make these judgments
  of life and death, of medical interventions,
  of division and distribution of my belongings.

I do not want to be in this place!
  Rage explodes in my heart.
  Angry tears burn my face.

And still, the decisions must be made.
  For I will not give my children this task.
  I will not set upon them terrible decisions.

The anger washes through my heart,
  spills upon the pages and slips away.
  Acceptance and resolve take its place.

And, so it is.

THE SACRED DANCE

Your soul calls, listen!
  You are not alone, ever!

Crying, sobbing, the pain
  as fresh as the first slash,
  blood, bright red, gushing.

Tears, hopelessness, fear.
  Alone, dark, no way out.
  Nightmare seething, here.

So many years, so much work,
  yet still, the horror grips me.
  Festering always, just below.

And still, I have no answers.
  Surrender, allow, feel, see.
  See into, beyond, through.

Spirit calls,
  'Let go the worn-out stories
  They deceive, distract, disturb.
  There is another truth, beneath.'

'Be quiet, breathe deeply, surrender.
  It is time to lay bare your wound.
  Allow the healing, feel the love.'

'Remember all you have learned.
  Know that you are never alone.
  Trust I AM your greater good.'

'Life, precious, wrapped, waiting.
  All you need do is surrender
  totally, allow. Then, witness

the Sacred Dance.'

THE EYE OF THE STORM

The moment in which I felt death upon me
  catalyzed a collision of events and introspection.

However, recently I entered a space of quiet.
  The gentle purr of my heart, the symptoms at bay...

'Perhaps,' I imagine, 'they were mistaken!'
  'Perhaps my heart is not, in fact, ailing!'

And then I smile at my ability for self-deception,
  and marvel at what really might be happening.

My prayers have been to remain healthy until
January, the date planned for the surgery.

A period of quiet in the storm is essential to
  delay healing my heart for such a long time.

And now, I find myself basking in that quiet!
  I have been gifted the time for which I prayed!

Succumbing to self-deception robs me of the chance
  to recognize and revel in the grace of prayers answered.

So, I pray each day that the veils be lifted from my sight,
  and give thanks for this exquisite gift, the eye of the storm.

JUST FEEL

In my meditation, a deep sadness permeated my being.
  I was lost in Briar Rabbit's burrow, far beneath the earth.
  The only sound, the crackle of brambles upon which I tread.

There was no fear in this place, no angst nor apprehension,
  no other emotions, in fact, aside from the profound sadness.
  The melancholy engulfed my heart and spilled from my eyes.

I recognized the trigger, an unforeseen call from a friend.
  'What is this sadness,' I asked. 'From where does it come?'
  I searched happenings, recent and past, to discover its origin.

But, I could find none that rose to claim title and deed.
  Struck by the depth of the sadness, I sought my friend.
  Each possible account I explored seemed awry, nihil ad rem.

The feeling lingers still, an eternal candle burning in my soul.
  It occurs to me that its apparent inscrutability is purposeful.
  Perhaps understanding is not the point at all, is nihil ad rem.

My mind relaxes its grip on its endeavor to understand.
  I re-orient my attention to quietly witness life unfolding.
  This morning, I am drawn to Wolf, sitting atop my alter.

It howls to the moon an aria of melancholy and sorrow.
  Alone it sits, a dark silhouette in the brilliant moonlight.
  Its heartfelt song fills the land, my heart, the dark of night.

Transfixed by the song, a tear escapes. Another follows.
  I feel. I simply feel the depths of the sadness, the hollows.
  Perhaps feeling the hollows is exactly what I am meant to do.

JOY BORN OF SORROW

Never, never is my intent to dishonor
or denigrate the devastating impact
of sorrow and oppression on a soul.

Yet, I continue to search for the meaning
of ideas gifted me with the concomitant
injunction to transmit their significance.

Experiences, mundane and momentous,
have been gifted for my enlightenment
on these matters of the soul embodied.

So, I petition them for another lesson.
I am ruminating on my ephemerality
on this plane, and in this incarnation.

I note nascent thoughts and feelings
and witness their journey through
my heart, mind, soul...this mortal.

I am witnessing how I attach meaning to new events,
namely through connections to previous experiences,
and how those attachments constrain my perception.

I was planning for the night prior to my heart surgery.
As I planned sleeping arrangements and our dinner,
I witnessed a sickening feeling quicken in my heart.

I followed that pain to a Thanksgiving long-past,
and the dinner my mother so flawlessly created
for her family, the eve before she started to die.

Sorrow, tears, mourning her death, my loss of her, still.
Serving dinner to my family on the eve of my surgery
retrieves this memory and reveals another attachment.

I remember that dinner and grieve her absence from my life.
But to attach the path of her life to my circumstance denies
me the precious experience of my own existence unfolding.

Recognizing this attachment, I can release it from my heart.
Free of the attachment, I can prepare dinner for my family
on the eve of my surgery to celebrate our love and my life.

Joy born of sorrow.

IT REALLY IS 'ALL ABOUT ME'

In the full throes of her awkward, impertinent adolescence,
  my daughter boldly wore a t-shirt, loudly proclaiming,
  'It's all about me!'

Us older and more mature adults looked on smugly.
  'It is all about her,' we smiled in our befuddled wisdom.
  And, we tiptoed around her audacious, immature call to self.

15-years later, I realize that, my child,
  in the freshness of her life on this planet,
  innately understood a fundamental fact of life.

It really is all about her...and me...and you...
  We are born to this world to explore our lives,
  to learn, to witness, to feel, to grow, to offer, to love.

We can't change circumstances into which we were born.
  Things happen in life that we didn't seek, but deeply feel.
  And, despite our valiant efforts, we cannot change another.

We can, however, decide how we will live
  in the circumstances into which we were born,
  through the things that happen throughout our lives.

Therein lie the gifts, the opportunities, the blessings
  endowed to us, created and offered for our ascendance.
  And always, we get to decide how we will answer the call.

The ascendance happens one person at a time,
  concerns one soul gifted with life upon this earth,
  is designed to craft the opportunities for her growth.

The changes, the real changes, the important changes,
  are those made inside ourselves, that then permeate us,
  and, through our living, spill from us to the life around us.

The abundance we generate through a life-practice of
  introspection, personal cleansing and growth issues from
  compassion-filled hearts to everything that we touch in life.

This is such a hard lesson to learn, though.
  It's so much easier to force change on another
  than to face and make the change required of self.

So easy is it to fall into the trap of other-focus,
  to smile smugly upon those who are less evolved,
  to strive toward their awakenings, even as we sleep.

Liberate from your closet your 'It's about me' T-shirt.
  Adorn yourself with it and bravely face your day, your self.
  Search inside to find your wondrous, enigmatic embodied-soul.

Settle into your own journey to ascendance.
  Seek, cleanse, create, love, learn, gift, witness, be.
  And remember, in the end, it really is all about you.

My Alakai

I query my 5-year old grandson,
  'How do you know there is wind?'
  Agile mind alert, he studies the forest.

'It makes the trees shake,' he says,
  and it makes all the leaves wriggle.'
  'But, you can't see wind,' I challenge.

'So, how do you know it is the wind?' I ask.
  He pauses, considering this knotty question.
  'Well,' he concludes, 'it makes my hair crazy,'
  tousling his hair with beautiful little boy hands.

Big eyes peer at me from beneath tousled hair.
  'Did I get it right?' they ask. We smile together.
  'Yes, you got it right! You are brilliant, my child!'
  Delighted, he exclaims, 'Nanna look! A baby deer!'

And our conversation supplely changes to plan the
  forts we will build next summer, because the deer
  need a place to sleep, and we plan to camp outside.

That's what we do, this beautiful boy and his Nanna.
  We go on adventures, in the world, and in our minds.
  There is much to see and do. We've no time to waste.

Here he comes now, soft-eyed and sleepy, for his hugs.
  We'll have pumpkin pie and hot chocolate for breakfast.
  And as this new day dawns, we'll plan our next adventure.

TORTOISE

The Tortoise requested to sit in the center
  of my alter, posed to see in all four directions.
  She can gaze down any path, but focuses on me.

She invites me into contemplation, to learn.
  With her great, slow strokes, she flies to the stars.
  I look upon her face and see eternity shining in her eyes.

Then, we are under water, her stroke unbroken.
  Her eyes wide, protected by a translucent sheath.
  In the dark, she sees clearly, swims steadily forward.

Again we are in the universe, surfing now on a planetary wave,
  flying around the moon, catching the crest of earth's gravity.
  The gravity unleashes its tether, casting us into the sun.

Into the sun's core we fall, flesh incinerated, Spirit released.
  Cleansed, we linger in the deep peace, One with the All.
  Ancients appear with a laser of light to etch on her shell.

They inscribe upon her back the wisdom of the ages,
  and send her forth to share the gift with all of humanity.
  To all corners of the earth, all of life, she carries the message.

She rests beneath still waters to glimpse the inscriptions
  in a reflection, and then swims on, for she is the messenger.
  She can't see, but fully comprehends, the wisdom she carries.

'Your life is a message,' Tortoise counsels me.
  'Allow the ancient wisdom to be inscribed upon you.
  'Let it emerge from your soul, then carry it for all to see.'

Like the Tortoise, we each have wisdom of the ages
  etched deeply upon our souls, visible to our mind's eye,
  a universal code of love to guide our walk through this life.

We need only to become quiet, to trust that the wisdom
  resides within each of us, that the wisdom is our heritage,
  and our connection to All, the ultimate and everlasting gift.

SURFACE REFLECTIONS

My contemplation these last months
  has been to witness all that emerges
  from within regarding my failing heart.

Many different emotions have surfaced.
  As children, they clamor for my attention.
  They want to be acknowledged and honored.

They want me to know them, to touch them.
  'Look at me!' they plead. 'Look at me, please.
  I am real. I have substance. I am important!'

'Please don't denounce me as unworthy or foul.
  Look upon me and see a reflection of your self.
  Hold me closely. Know my depths and expanse.'

'Experience me as a lover, child, teacher.
  Don't obscure me with the inane chatter
  of your highly-educated, benighted mind.'

'Quiet your mind and witness me, just me.
  Strip away the attachments, the judgments,
  and see me, unadulterated, naked, remarkable.'

'I simply am. I exist. I am worthy. I am you.
  I am anger. I am sadness. I am joy. I am you.
  I am concern. I am fear. I am gratitude. I am you.'

'I ask your undivided attention. I show you me.
  Thankful, reassured, elated when you honor me,
  I return to the eternal reservoir of tranquility in you.'

I want to allow and honor these many emotions
  because they show me who I am in this passing.
  They rise and fall, surge and swell as ocean waves.

And beneath them all, there flows a reservoir,
  deep beyond imagination, expanding to forever,
  of tranquility, the peace that passes understanding.

It is the source of all knowing, all being, All.
  You are its progeny, its beloved, its promise.
  It is the wellspring of hope, grace, compassion.

And, it flows through your being, is of you.
  Tranquil amidst storms raging in your heart.
  Offering sanctuary, serenity, harmony, always.

WISDOM EMBODIED

The awkward and uncertain gait of
  a bumbling human carrying a wise soul.

That's the title of my life,
  the music filling the setting
  of the stage on which I play.

The soul is wisdom, grace and beauty.
  And it chose to walk with me,
  little me, through this life.

I am awkward in my movements,
  fall when attempting to walk,
  subvert myself as I reach to forever,
  seek refuge in worn-out stories,
  prefer the dark to the light...

Yet, my soul perseveres,
  vigilant in its encouragement,
  always watchful of my journey,
  until the finish, my companion.

For as flawed as my attempts to live,
  or my understanding of how to be,
  my soul needs me.

The struggles that drop me to my knees,
  the tears that burn my cheeks,
  the joy that fills my heart...

all these humble attempts to be human
  gift my soul with the lessons it
  embodied to experience.

So, next I see you,
  and when inevitably
  I stumble and fall...

Please know that
  inside this bumbling human
  laughs a magnificent soul!

IT IS JUST ENOUGH

54 years and 4 months. 19,831 days.
  All these days, I have walked this sacred path.
  All these days, I have been gifted on this journey.

I am so profoundly grateful,
  for every moment, every breath,
  for every smile, every tear, even fear.

I accept the rising sun, my birth,
  and the setting moon, my quietus,
  and the star reborn, my transfiguration.

I am at peace with what may come.
  I live, aware, witnessing, experiencing,
  reaching out and up and beyond to the All.

It is just enough.

IN THE PRESENCE OF THE DIVINE

I realized yesterday that I am done
  contemplating the upcoming surgery.

Just like that and for no particular reason,
  I'm done. I am at peace with the surgery.
  And, I am done contemplating my mortality.

I don't know what spiritual/emotional boundary
  I crossed, nor do I remember passing through it.
  But, I realize I am on the other side, and at peace.

I am at peace with all the days apportioned to this life.
  I accept whatever outcomes emerge from the surgery.
  I honor the sanctity of life, on and beyond this plane.

The moment I recognized this shift, I felt a sense of
  gratitude for the many blessings showered upon
  me in this lifetime, a reverence, euphoria, awe.

I am standing in the presence of the Divine.
  Everything is exactly as it is meant to be.
  I am asked to quiet my mind and heart.

Now, bear witness to a sacred dance.
  The Divine breathes, life moves.

PIERCING THE SURFACE

There is a deeper gratitude that I am asked to feel.
It transcends thankfulness for that which I desired.
Its tendrils penetrate the dark, musty soil of my being.
In that rich, thick loam rest the seeds of my ascendance.

My transgressions, my heart-wrenching anguish, my dolor,
those who summoned demons of anger and enmity in me,
all the painful, gruesome, ghastly moments I experienced,
the dark, restless, never-happy, ungrateful, obdurate self...

ALL these were gifts, given with the deepest of love, to me.
Life's sweet irony, the exquisite and remarkable stories I live.
The pristine bloom does not magically appear to grace life.
It is born, nourished and protected in the dank, murky soul.

So too, our lives.

My gratitude emerges from a realization that via the trials,
I have been offered innumerable opportunities to grow,
to feel Divine grace, to glimpse and remember eternity,
to witness miracles, to find the wisdom I seek inside me.

HOLDING VIGIL

As I passed through the dark of my home this morning,
I felt the presence of many souls watching me from outside.
I felt their frantic, desperate need to reach me from beyond.

I stood before them, square feet, broad shoulders,
my arms drawn across my chest, my stance strong.
Threatened, I declared, 'You may not enter here!'

I cleansed the house, blocking their entrance into my space.
As I stood strong before the window, I saw a small statue
of an African woman holding vigil over an eternal flame.

The spirit of Africa flows through her, touches my soul,
carries me to Zimbabwe, the land where heaven touches
the earth and voices of the dead echo across the savanna.

'So many souls, so much pain, so eager to release the pain,
so thirsty for compassion, so hungry for love,' she whispers.
'Don't drive them away. Embrace them, fill them with love.'

'They seek you because you can see, you can help,' she says.
'There is only fear and love. With love, there can be no fear.
Gift love, melt fear with kindness. Keep vigil for all, always.'

BE

Sometimes, I feel the air about me tingling, sparkling.
Like each atom is dancing in delight and expectation.
The energy permeates every pore, floods my body.
Waves rush through me, bursting from my head.
There is a party going on, hosted by life itself.
All are welcomed, material and incorporeal.
All are asked to awaken from the slumber.
Shake off the malaise of mere existence.
Feel the ecstasy of Qi surging, flowing.
Know the quintessence of Qi is love.
Wake up to the wonder that is you.
Revel in the glory, magnificence.
Then, stand, sing and dance.
You are gifted with this life.
Live each moment fully,
with gusto and passion.
Breath deeply the Qi.
Exhale, inhale, live.
This gift for you,
exquisite love.
Awaken now.
Allow. Feel
the spark.
Rejoice
Dance
Love
Be.

ABOUT THE AUTHOR

I feel 'all talked out'. But, there is more. I can feel Spirit's call once again. So, I dive back into life to discover the gems of wisdom hidden in the ever-so-ordinary daily walk.

Namaste!

INDEX

Made in the USA
Columbia, SC
23 March 2018